The Hike
into the Sun

The Hike into the Sun

Memoir of an American Soldier Captured on Bataan in 1942 and Imprisoned by the Japanese until 1945

BERNARD T. FITZPATRICK
with John A. Sweetser III

McFarland & Company, Inc., Publishers
Jefferson, North Carolina, and London

The present work is a reprint of the library bound edition of The
Hike into the Sun: Memoir of an American Soldier Captured on Bataan in 1942 and Imprisoned by the Japanese
until 1945, first published in 1993 by McFarland.

Unless otherwise attributed, photographs are from the collection
of Bernard T. FitzPatrick.

LIBRARY OF CONGRESS CATALOGUING-IN-PUBLICATION DATA

FitzPatrick, Bernard T.
    The hike into the sun : memoir of an American soldier cap-
tured on Bataan in 1942 and imprisoned by the Japanese until
1945 / Bernard T. FitzPatrick with John A. Sweetser III.
        p.   cm.
    Includes bibliographical references and index.

    ISBN 978-0-7864-6776-1
    softcover : 50# alkaline paper ∞

    1. FitzPatrick, Bernard T.   2. Bataan (Philippines :
Province), Battle of, 1942.   3. World War, 1939–1945—
Prisoners and prisons, Japanese.   4. World War, 1939–1945—
Personal narratives, American.   5. Prisoners of War—United
States—Biography.   6. Prisoners of war—Philippines—
Biography.   7. Prisoners of war—Japan—Biography.
8. United States. Army—Biography.   I. Sweetser, John A.,
1919–1998.   II. Title.
D767.4.F6 2011
915.8'50485—dc20   92-56641

BRITISH LIBRARY CATALOGUING DATA ARE AVAILABLE

Front cover: Near the end of the Bataan Death March in Philippines,
1942 (Library of Congress); background © 2011 Shutterstock

Manufactured in the United States of America

McFarland & Company, Inc., Publishers
    Box 611, Jefferson, North Carolina 28640
        www.mcfarlandpub.com

This book is dedicated to
the men of the 194th Tank Battalion,
the first armored unit ever to leave
the United States to go overseas

CONTENTS

MAPS AND ILLUSTRATIONS

Maps

Illustrations

ACKNOWLEDGMENTS

*T*HE AUTHORS would like to thank J. B. Sisson, for his editorial contribution, and Kevin FitzPatrick, for his overall involvement in the making of this book. They would also like to thank their wives, Corinne FitzPatrick and Druanne Sweetser, and other family members and friends who have provided help, insight, and encouragement.

They are also grateful to Ben Steele, professor of art emeritus at Eastern Montana College, for the use of his drawings in this book. A survivor of the Bataan Death March and prison camps in the Philippines and Japan, he began his career as an artist by drawing as a war prisoner in Bilibid Prison in Manila while he was immobilized by illness. His drawings presented in this book, with the exception of "Noon Fight Over Food," have been selected from his collection of drawings, *Prisoner of War* (Department of Art, Eastern Montana College, Billings, 1986).

Finally, thanks to Brian Kowalski and Steve Leach of the Cartography Lab of the Geography Department of the University of Minnesota for the maps that appear in this book.

INTRODUCTION
Hospital Train Homeward

EARLY NOVEMBER 1945: I stared out of the window of the hospital train, as excited as a boy opening Christmas presents. Liberated from a Japanese prisoner-of-war camp, I was back in the United States, and everything I saw was a curiosity. Automobiles on the streets, haircuts, fashions, even women in uniforms—Wacs and Waves—were all new to me. What planet had I been on for nearly four years? The other former war prisoners gawked too as we departed from Madigan General Hospital near Tacoma, Washington, and saw shoppers peering into store windows. We jabbered to each other in "bamboo Japanese," trying to figure out what the shoppers were doing. Our hospital-train attendants had been shaking their heads ever since we boarded, not understanding our mixture of English and Japanese with a *u* sound tagged to the ends of many English words: *wifu, housu, knifu, forku, cupu, bucketsu*. We'd say "changie-changie" when we were trading among ourselves. All of us had been captured at Bataan or Corregidor and had shared a harrowing fellowship. Those of us in Bataan had been on the long forced march to a prison camp, a brutal experience we called the Hike. Only later, when we returned to the United States, would we hear it called the Bataan Death March.

On the hospital train we were ordered to turn in our uniforms for pajamas. Debilitated as we were, most of us were young and like wild horses in spring, and pajamas were the army's way of corralling us. Our destination was not home but Schick General Hospital in Clinton, Iowa, where we would spend months recuperating before being discharged. I had weighed 175 pounds when I was drafted in April 1941, and when I was released from prison camp in September 1945 I weighed 104 pounds. My prison-camp illnesses included malaria, pellagra, jaundice, tuberculosis, beriberi, filariasis, corneal ulcers, dysentery, scurvy, and what is now called post-traumatic stress syndrome.

1

The mortality rate for war prisoners in Japanese camps was dramatically higher than for war prisoners in German camps. Not only were we physically deprived for several years but our Japanese captors called us *horyo*, a term that can be translated as "vicious criminals," "the lowest of the low," or "dishonored captives." The Japanese did not believe in honorable surrender. Of the 10,000 American soldiers who began the Bataan Death March, only 1,100 survived the march and the following three and a half years in prison camp. The concept of *horyo* and the consequent mistreatment were part of the cultural differences I observed between Japanese and American worldviews.

We traveled the Great Northern route back to the Midwest, on the tracks that James J. Hill completed from St. Paul to Seattle a little over 50 years before. We returned through forests and pastures, mountains and plains, harvested hay and wheat fields, through Washington, Idaho, Montana, and North Dakota, finally descending toward St. Paul, Minnesota. During most of our three-day train ride, we told stories about our experiences, sang, and simply gazed out of the window. We stayed up all night talking and caught catnaps during the day. I was so used to sleeping on the ground that I was uncomfortable sleeping on the train. At the Madigan hospital many of us had slept on the floor with only a blanket.

One night as we sang, one of the men broke into "Dugout Doug, come out from hiding, / Send to Franklin these glad tidings / That his troops go starving on!" I was surprised how many of the soldiers knew the lyrics. Before the fall of Bataan, Jerry Lundquist and I had written the words of "Dugout Doug," anonymously, to vent our frustration at General Douglas MacArthur's way of conducting the American military operation. The lyrics were set to the tune of the "Battle Hymn of the Republic." We had been on half rations or less for four months before we were captured, and we were very short on medical supplies, especially quinine, as well as ammunition and military maintenance equipment. Had we suffered and died because of inept military policy and leadership? Since we were still in the army, we discussed this question discreetly both in prison camp and on the trip home, but I have continued to study this issue through the decades.

Our bull sessions and singing on the train reminded me of our 24-day trip on the hospital ship, the *Klipfontein*, from Manila to Seattle in October 1945. Our storytelling flowed easily as we stood at the rail overlooking the moonlit Pacific. More than 1,000 former war prisoners

Bernard FitzPatrick, 1946, after many months of hospitalization.

and refugees from all points of the Far East were on board this con-verted ocean liner. One soldier, R. D. Russell from Texas, said that I had remembered so much that I should write a book. His remark echoed in my mind two decades later, in 1967, when I returned to the Philippines and Japan for the twenty-fifth anniversary of the fall of Bataan. Sitting around a table in the bar of a Manila hotel, talking and singing with other former war prisoners, I was urged by Burt Ellis to write my stories down so they would not be lost.

Writing a book soon after the war wasn't possible, but the seeds were planted then as I relaxed on the *Klipfontein*. On board I met two people who were working on books already. Agnes Newton Keith, the author of the widely read *Land Below the Wind*, was writing *Three Came Home*, about her Japanese prison experience in Borneo. Dr. Alfred A. Weinstein, an army surgeon and a war prisoner with me in Cabana-tuan, had begun writing *Barbed-Wire Surgeon*.

I was saddened to hear from Dr. Weinstein that Father Theodore Buttenbruch, S.V.D., a German citizen living in Manila, had been killed by the Japanese. Our spirits had always lifted when we saw his battered old truck driving toward our prison compound. He scoured

Manila for vegetables, pineapples, papayas, candy, books, and toilet articles for refugees and American soldiers. At first the Japanese let him travel freely because of his German citizenship, and at first we distrusted him. But he relayed many messages from the outside, including messages from Dr. Weinstein's future wife, Hanna Kaunitz, a Viennese refugee who had arrived in Manila in 1938. Father Buttenbruch was tireless in his protest against our ill-treatment. In the end, as the Japanese made their last stand in Manila in February 1945, he was tortured, beheaded, and dismembered.

Over the years, in reading about the Second World War in the Philippines, I have been troubled by how little credit has been given to people like Father Buttenbruch and the many Filipinos who risked their lives to help American prisoners by such acts as providing a cup of water to a dehydrated soldier during the Bataan Death March. Men such as Dr. Mariano Marfori and Dr. Ricardo de Guzman and women such as Maria Ravelo worked courageously to restore us to health. And there were Japanese soldiers and civilians who helped us as much as they could under the iron-cruel system of the Japanese Imperial Army. Captain Wakamori and Sergeant Teramura treated us humanely, and Colonel Imai refused to carry out a direct order to kill his prisoners on Bataan.

I had been in no hurry to get to Tacoma and more confinement at Madigan General Hospital. Morris Doerfler, a member of the army air corps, had managed to reserve some seats on a plane to the United States, and he had invited Bill McKeon and me to go with him. I had grown up with Morris in Waverly, Minnesota, a small farming town 40 miles west of Minneapolis, and we had survived the Death March and prison camp together. I thanked Morris but told him I had enough food now and no one was poking me with a stick or a rifle butt, so I was content to find the biggest ship available and lie down. Bill McKeon agreed with me.

In fact, I was a bit more active on the *Klipfontein*. I was asked to be an announcer on the ship's radio station, probably because of my wartime experience in radio communications, my relatively uncluttered English, and my background in music—I was a leader of the glee club and choir in prison camp. I dubbed it Radio XPOW and made announcements, read news, and played records. Soldiers restricted to the hospital ward would hoot and holler when I played "Don't Fence Me In." When I was feeling cocky and in good voice, I'd sing.

On our train to the hospital in Iowa I wondered if we would stop in St. Paul. Before I was drafted, I had lived in St. Paul, having graduated from the College of St. Thomas and begun a career in insurance there. My mother Catherine, a widow in her mid-sixties, had moved to St. Paul from Waverly to spend the winter with my sister Florence and help her with her two babies. And I was not the only one who was clamoring for the train to stop . Many of the survivors of the Bataan Death March were members of the 194th Tank Battalion stationed at Brainerd–Fort Ripley, Minnesota. The hospital-train commander was a young doctor from St. Paul, John Fee, who was friendly, generous, and careful in his attention to the medical problems of the soldiers on board. In Fargo, North Dakota, with a little more persuasion from me, Dr. Fee wired army headquarters, and a three-hour leave was approved for all of us. We turned in our pajamas for uniforms. We looked like soldiers when the train entered the St. Paul depot. At Madigan General Hospital an auxiliary of older women called Gray Ladies had helped us sew on chevrons and insignias and position our medals properly.

My mother was waiting for me as we disembarked from the train. She was crying. I had wired her from Manila that I was alive. That was the first she had heard from me since I was captured three and a half years before. She had thought I was dead because a war prisoner who had arrived home earlier had reported that I had died on a prison ship transporting me to Japan. As we drove to my sister Florence's house, my mother told me she had received my telegram as she came out of church on a Friday morning in Waverly. She was alone at the top of the steps as the Western Union man hurried up toward her. My mother could barely speak. "Are you bringing me good news?" she asked. The man smiled and said yes and read the telegram.

But the joy of our meeting now in St. Paul was tempered by the report that Morris Doerfler was presumed dead. I had heard at the Madigan hospital that his flight was missing, and my mother confirmed this news. Morris had sent a telegram to his parents that he was on his way home, but the plane was lost over the Pacific.

Our three-hour visit seemed over in a few minutes, and I was soon back at the St. Paul train station. I expected to find everyone milling around, but the station was deserted. Across the street I saw Dr. Fee with two nurses hurrying into Sugar's Bar. Sugar's Bar had been a watering hole for train travelers for years. I followed behind at an inconspicuous distance. Bedlam roared inside as many of my fellow war prisoners were flapping their freedom with a little unruly fun. Some of them had been drinking for three hours and were now wrestling at the bar and on top of the pool tables and yelling in bamboo Japanese. They relished calling one another a blankety-blank baka, a person without brains, the worst insult a Japanese soldier could receive. Two soldiers with samurai swords were taking good-natured swipes at the bartender whenever he objected to the horseplay. Broken furniture littered the floor.

Calm was eventually restored as Dr. Fee and the nurses waded in. Most of the men got back on the train. A number of them, however, missed the departure and straggled down to Schick General Hospital over the next week. Dr. Fee soon found himself assigned to Germany. A few years later, my wife Corinne and I bought a house across the street from him in St. Paul. One Saturday as I was raking leaves, he gave me the business for talking him into a lot of hot water with his military superiors for those three hours at Sugar's Bar.

At Schick General Hospital I met war prisoners and old friends Sergeant Myron Hayes and Staff Sergeant Ed Wright. From them I learned that Lieutenant Larry Hendrickson was killed on a prison ship. Corporal LeRoy Little was seriously ill in Fitzsimmons Hospital. I would be a pallbearer for LeRoy the next June. All of these men grew up in small towns near Waverly.

After a thorough checkup at Schick, I was given a ten-day leave, and I returned to Minnesota. On a downtown St. Paul street I ran into a relative of a soldier who had died in prison camp. We began a discreet dance of words, a dance in which I would participate often over the years, in person, by letter, or by phone with other relatives, mothers, fathers, wives, and children. It is a dance I am a partner in to this day, half a century later. Indirectly, the family member would ask me how the relative died. I would tell what happened truthfully but as gently as possible. For example, if a soldier died of "natural causes," I would cite the specific disease, but I wouldn't say that the disease was a starvation disease, that in fact he had starved to death.

I preferred to describe the courage and camaraderie that the war prisoners had exhibited throughout their captivity. I emphasized this aspect a few days later when I visited the parents of Morris Doerfler. They were hardworking German dairy farmers. It was one of the most difficult visits I ever made. They were consoled to hear that after the

Death March, Morris had worked as a stevedore in Manila Harbor and was under a decent Japanese officer. He had had enough to eat, and he had gone out of his way to load and unload extra cargo when a fellow war prisoner was too sick to work.

For years I corresponded with Mrs. Magruder G. Maury, the mother of Major Thompson Brooke Maury, a West Point graduate who was captured on Bataan and died when the unmarked "hell ship" taking him to Japan was bombed by American planes. In every letter she asked for recollections to include in a biography she was writing for the family. The Maurys were an old, distinguished Virginia family. She was grateful to hear of Major Maury's care of the men under him. Major Maury voluntarily walked the march out of Bataan, when he could have ridden with the staff officers of his unit. During the Death March he intervened bodily when a bayonet-wielding Japanese soldier was threatening a sick, lagging American. Mrs. Maury was comforted to know he sang in the glee club and, though he was not Catholic, sang with us Montani's *Missa Brevis*, a mass he loved to hear. Major Maury greatly admired Shakespeare, and I told Mrs. Maury how I appreciated his reading aloud and dramatizing difficult passages in *King Lear*. Father Buttenbruch had given us a copy of Shakespeare's plays, and Major Maury's presentations were edifying and entertaining. He literally foamed from the mouth for one of Lear's soliloquies.

Another mother sometimes drove 100 miles from rural Minnesota to visit me in my insurance office in downtown St. Paul. She would sit in my office for 15 to 20 minutes and say very little, comforted because I had known her son and was with him when he died.

After the months of recuperation at Schick General Hospital, I was released to the outpatient clinic at the Veterans Hospital in Minneapolis with a disability rating of 100 percent. Before returning to Minnesota, I was honorably discharged at Fort Sheridan, Illinois, in May 1946. My rank was sergeant. I stopped in Chicago on my way back. The changes in American life were still new and confusing to me. On my last day in Chicago I was stuck in a traffic jam on the way to the train station. A crowd of screaming teenage girls blocked my taxi. I asked the driver what was going on. He told me matter-of-factly that the girls were bobby-soxers trying to get a glimpse of Frank Sinatra, who was staying at a nearby hotel. "What are bobby-soxers?" I asked. "Who's Frank Sinatra?"

Part One

THE HIKE

1

DEBACLE AT CLARK FIELD

A T CLARK FIELD on the Philippine island of Luzon, 55 miles
northwest of Manila, the 194th Tank Battalion had been on war
alert since December 1, 1941. Our commanding officer, Major Ernest B.
Miller, a veteran of the First World War, had positioned our tanks and
half-tracks on the north and east sides of Clark Field, barely concealed
in the tall, dry cogon grass. Our mission was to repel or destroy the
Japanese paratroopers who were expected to be dropped after a bombing attack. It was 6:30 on the morning of December 8, 1941 (December
7, Hawaiian time). I could not believe the announcement: "The
Japanese have just bombed Pearl Harbor." Most of the men could not
believe the Japanese would be so foolish. We assumed that the attack
had been easily brushed aside. After all, Pearl Harbor was so well
armed.

So I stood by the tank of which I was a crew member, and I looked
up at the clear, fresh morning sky. To the west the peaks of the
Zambales Mountains stood out clearly. Through the concealing fringe
of cogon grass, I watched the P-40 fighters and then the B-17 bombers
start down the strip, take off into the gentle wind from the west, and
curve up into formations headed north. We listened to the messages
on the big radio receiver and transmitter in the half-track that served
as the command-post communication center. My tank was only a few
yards from this radio half-track, and most of the messages were "in the
clear"—not coded or even guardedly cryptic.

A little after 9:00 A.M. a message came in from Clark Field headquarters that the Japanese had bombed Aparri, at the northern tip of
Luzon, and Davao, on the south coast of Mindanao—two attacks,
about 1,000 miles apart. We hardly knew more than the names of the
places. After a few more minutes—it was beginning to be warm in the
cogon grass out of the slight wind—another announcement crackled

11

out on the loudspeakers of the half-track. Baguio and Camp John Hay, only 100 miles north of us, had been bombed.

We waited. The day grew warmer. At about 10:30 the planes began to return. The P-40s and the B-17s landed and taxied into the neat lines of dress parade. The line of B-17s ended close to us. One plane was only about 35 feet from my tank. The prop wash of the planes blew dust through the cogon grass to us, and then the engines were silent. We could hear the messages on the radio again. We could hear the pilots and their crews talking near their planes.

At about noon a message came through from Colonel James R. N. Weaver, the tank-group commander at the air corps headquarters at Clark Field. There was an all clear: tank crews could go to their mess halls for lunch. But despite Colonel Weaver's message, Major Miller immediately spoke on the battalion intercom: "All members of the 194th Tank Battalion will stand by their vehicles. I repeat, all members of the 194th. . . ."

So we waited and watched the pilots and the bomber crews walking across the field to their mess halls. I saw Major Miller at the command post next to the radio half-track, talking hurriedly but privately to his intelligence officer, Captain F. G. Spoor. Spoor saluted, climbed into a jeep, and motioned to the driver. The jeep left at top speed across the field toward headquarters.

The air grew hotter. We could hear music. One of the tank crews had become bored and had switched their radio to KZRH, a commercial station in Manila. The music was interrupted, and Don Bell of KZRH announced excitedly that Clark Field was being bombed. It was then 12:25 P.M. It was quiet and warm, and the Zambales Mountains were blue in the early afternoon haze. We all felt confused and wanted to laugh.

Five minutes later an orange amphibious airplane lumbered down into a landing on the runway nearest us. It slowed to a stop just off the edge of the runway, and the crew and some passengers jumped down from the plane and began to run for the other side of the field. At least two of the passengers carried attaché cases. I turned and looked up in the sky to the north. The sky seemed to be full of small, silver-colored planes headed toward us. I turned to Lieutenant A. Hook, our tank commander, and said, "Look at our navy planes." "How do you know they're navy planes?" he replied. "Because our army planes are grayish green."

"The Bombing of Clark Field," a drawing by Ben Steele.

A swishing, rumbling sound cut through our talk, and Major Miller yelled over the intercom, "Take cover!"

Lieutenant Hook and I dove under our tank. The exploding bombs drove consciousness into some recess of the brain. The ear-shattering noise and the shaking of the ground became one sensation, joined by other kinds of explosions—gas tanks and ammunition igniting.

After a short while, in a lull, we looked out from under the front of our tank. Fires and smoke were everywhere, but the B-17s were still there on dress parade. Then came the Japanese planes that we learned later were Zeros. They were working over everything missed by the bombers, paying special attention to the B-17s. Lieutenant Hook and I lay on the ground watching, fascinated. While strafing the B-17s, one silver Zero, with the red sun insignia on the underside of each wing, seemed right over us. The nearest B-17 exploded and disintegrated as the Zero passed. The accuracy of the bombing and strafing was frightening.

Then, again and again, the Zeros strafed the bomb trailers lined up at the far end of the field. That evening I learned why the Japanese pilots paid such careful attention to those empty trailers. Domei News on Radio Tokyo announced triumphantly that the 194th Tank "Division" had been destroyed during the attack on Clark Field. We laughed at that, but it was cold comfort. In less than an hour the Japanese had destroyed half of our air force in the Philippines, the last serious deterrent to Japanese conquest of most of the Pacific. Japan would have the Pacific to herself for almost two years.

After the strafers had made their last run, with practically every visible target blown up or on fire, our men began to straggle out of their hiding places, from under tanks or half-tracks. Some were so dazed that they were walking in circles. A couple of small fires in the cogon grass were beaten out. Right behind our tanks were open stores of bombs and gasoline. Just one Japanese bomb or one strafer slightly off his target and we would have been smoked out of hiding. The dead and wounded of other units were all around us. Because of Major Miller's tough sense of duty and his intuition, he had ordered the tank battalion to stand by when the all clear was sounded, and so our losses that day were minimal: only one killed and three wounded.

Captain Spoor returned to the command post after the bombing and reported to Major Miller. He had found the tank-group commander, Colonel Weaver, and had spent some time with him giving Major Miller's arguments as to why the 194th should stand by. While talking to Colonel Weaver, Captain Spoor overheard an order from General Douglas MacArthur's Manila headquarters of the U.S. Armed Forces of the Far East (USAFFE): the planes on Clark Field were ordered to remain on the ground. The bombing started a few minutes afterward.

Late in the afternoon Major Miller had the field kitchen units cook us a hot meal and serve it to us in small groups. He did not want us to leave our positions, and most of the mess halls had been destroyed. He abolished rank for the mess line: every man, regardless of rank, would be served in the order of arrival. The morale of the 194th shot up further.

That night Major Miller was ordered to place three tanks on the Clark Field runways in case of a paratrooper attack. The tank I was assigned to was positioned right in the middle of Clark Field. I was unable to sleep, so I kept watch until the night of December 10. Then I slept on the ground next to the tank for 12 hours.

Shortly after noon on December 10 I saw a single B-17 bomber come in over Clark Field from the north, pursued by a Zero. The Japanese fighter repeatedly curved up and fired at the belly of the B-17. We watched until both planes were out of sight. A few minutes later we heard on the communication half-track radio at the command post an excited message from one of our outpost half-tracks southeast of us near Mount Arayat. Sergeant Long was asking for permission to repel an attack by Japanese paratroopers. He was told to fire at will. The supposed paratroopers were really the crew of the B-17 that had just passed overhead. When the B-17 was about to crash, the pilot, Captain Colin Kelly, had stayed with the plane to give his crew a chance to bail out.

After the war I learned that the Zero pilot who had shot down this B-17 was Japan's greatest surviving war ace, Saburo Sakai. The war-crimes commission in Tokyo, acting on false information, charged Saburo Sakai with wantonly shooting at the crew of Colin Kelly's plane after they had bailed out. Some of our tank-group personnel at Clark Field who had seen the incident testified on Saburo Sakai's behalf. He had run out of ammunition, but, impressed by the B-17's toughness, speed, and maneuverability, he had flown close to take photos of the plane. Then he had swerved off and flown back to Formosa.

The Japanese bombers and the Zeros came again on two more raids after December 8. They did not realize how complete had been the destruction of the first raid, and they worked over our barracks and the few remaining buildings. The ruins smoldered for days.

2

INTO THE BREACH

O N THE NIGHT of December 12 we of the 194th Tank Battalion
were uprooted from our positions at Mabalacat, just north of
Clark Field. General MacArthur's headquarters ordered us to make a
night march to the Calumpit bridges south of us on the road to
Manila. In the early evening, already dark from a heavy, overcast sky,
amidst a thin, chilly drizzle we started down Route 3 with 162 vehicles:
54 light tanks and 19 half-tracks, along with trucks, jeeps, reconnaissance cars, and motorcycles. The move was difficult because all
traffic in the Philippines drove on the left-hand side of the road. We
were driving under blackout conditions, with only the faintest blue-
green light from the painted-over headlights. That eerie glow was swallowed up by the mist and drizzle three feet in front of the vehicles.

Our tank driver was Private First Class Specialist Kenny Gordon,
and Private First Class Specialist Jim Bogart was the machine gunner
and assistant driver. They were both from Brainerd, Minnesota.
Lieutenant A. Hook from Salinas, California, was our tank commander as well as platoon leader, and I operated radio communications. Our radios were effective up to about two miles, and then I
switched to key operations. Because of the constant jostling and vibration inside a tank—it was like being crammed into a small boiler
factory—I often had to convey incoming messages with hand and foot
signals.

Coming up the road from Manila, also mainly without lights, was
a steady stream of buses, trucks, carts drawn by the water buffalo called
carabao, and refugees on foot. From then on, until the final stand at
Bataan, we became accustomed to roads clogged with uprooted people
fleeing in every direction.

There were quite a few minor accidents as tanks and trucks slipped
into ditches or made a wrong turn and wandered off in the darkness

toward Bataan. One tank overturned, but luckily no one was hurt on that long night. Our tanks weighed more than 14 tons and were designed to travel through rough, off-the-road terrain such as trails, logs, rocks, and open hills. Inside, we bounced and rolled as in the barrel ride at the state fair. During training I learned to secure my crash helmet tight, after banging my head against the side of a tank.

By daylight the next morning the entire battalion was in bivouac positions, awkwardly strung out in three scattered spots, because there was so little cover to hide all our vehicles and equipment from the air. The area of the Calumpit bridges had few trees and many rice paddies. A tank or truck could operate no more than a few feet from the road. The new day dawned clear and bright. The daylight showed us how poor the cover was: tall bushes rather than trees. Major Miller, chewing on his ever-present cigar, kept looking up at the Japanese planes, which flew over us all day long but made no attempt to bomb us.

Early the next day we got the whole convoy back on the road in small groups. We had good visibility and attracted no attention from the Japanese planes. When we reached Manila, most of us were too tired and too busy driving in the dust and heat to notice much. That evening we bivouacked under heavy groves of mango trees in Muntinlupa, about 15 miles south of Manila.

For the next ten days I slept next to the tank along with Kenny Gordon and the rest of the crew. In the cool evenings we were grateful for the heavy-duty canvas sleeping bags we had bought at the post exchange back at Fort Stotsenburg, near Clark Field. We learned that we were then attached to the Southern Luzon Force, though still under the direct command of USAFFE—a tactically and administratively cumbersome arrangement that would cost us before we were done.

At this time some officers in our battalion were promoted, and Major Miller became a lieutenant colonel. During those ten days of inactivity he and his executive officer, Major Charles Canby, sent out reconnaissance groups every day to scout this part of southern Luzon where none of us had been before. No guides were sent to us. The only maps in the whole battalion were three outdated maps. One was legitimately issued to Miller after a great deal of strenuous effort and paperwork, and the other two were acquired at USAFFE headquarters by the clandestine tactics of Captain Spoor and Captain Johnson. In that lotus-eating time before the war, only four maps of the Philippines had been made: one of the whole Philippine Islands, one of the main islands, and two of parts of the island of Luzon. Only one of the Luzon maps, issued by blueprint process in very small numbers, was useful for military purposes. This map showed trails that no longer existed. So the reconnaissance missions returned dog tired from 50-mile trips, south to Batangas, east around Laguna de Bay, and east and south to Candelaria. Each day they returned with overlay maps to guide the battalion in the southern Luzon area.

In the evenings and on through the nights Colonel Miller kept a careful guard on the bivouac area. Unauthorized lights were suspiciously frequent, and, with warnings from the local constabulary, the guards shot them out. A certain woman showed up too often and asked too many questions. She was politely taken to Manila and handed over to intelligence at USAFFE, but there was no proof that she was a spy. She was released, and she showed up all smiles at our bivouac again. Captain Spoor handed over the next suspicious visitor to the constabulary, who kept him out of the way until after we had left the area.

On December 24 new orders came from USAFFE through the tank-group commander, now Brigadier General James Weaver. Company C was to remain there and serve under General Albert M. Jones, commanding the South Luzon Force. The rest of us were sent north through Manila all the way to Carmen, on the Agno River twenty miles south of Lingayen Gulf, where the main force of the Japanese 14th Army, commanded by General Masaharu Homma, had invaded on December 22. There had been little resistance at Lingayen Gulf, and the Japanese forces were now heading south to take Manila.

Again we were off to an area that we had not been able to scout, and we had neither proper maps nor guides. We had been through Carmen only on one prewar road march. As we passed back through Manila, each platoon stopped, and men were sent to get maps from the local gas stations. My tank had a Standard Oil map. It covered the main highways but of course was no help with the back roads or trails.

My platoon stopped near the Manila Hotel, a posh preserve for the wealthy of Manila and the high-ranking military officers. General MacArthur and his family lived in the hotel penthouse, although he had already begun to move his headquarters to the island of Corregidor. I had nothing to do while we waited for the men to return with the road maps, so I hunted up our company commander, Captain Ed Burke, and said I would like to visit the Manila Hotel. He laughed, looking at my tank coveralls and crash helmet, and said, "Go ahead." We both thought I wouldn't get beyond the doorman. Captain Burke had recommended me for officer training, and I had been scheduled to return to the United States on December 18, but the outbreak of war canceled that plan.

I walked across the street and through the ornate entrance and into the bar. No one paid any attention to me. Although no one was at the bar, all the tables were filled with men and women. I stepped up to the bar and asked the bartender for a drink. He didn't blink an eye. "How about a little bourbon and charged water, soldier," he said.

I nodded and, putting my crash helmet on the bar, I started to pull some money out of my pockets.

He put up his hand and grinned. "This one is on the house, soldier."

I bought a second drink and looked around at the men in white tropical suits and the women in long dresses. They seemed a bit subdued. On the bar was a copy of the December 24 *Manila Times*, with headlines screaming "MacArthur Takes the Field" and an article about the Japanese 14th Army pushing down from Lingayen Gulf toward Manila.

The people behind me at the nearest table were talking about the invasion. One woman asked a man, "What are we going to do?"

He said confidently, "It's no problem. We've recently been heavily reinforced with soldiers from the United States, like those at the bar."

I looked up from my drink, right and then left: I was the only person at the bar. The Philippines were in big trouble. I had a third drink, sketched a salute to the bartender, and went back out into the afternoon sunlight to rejoin my platoon. In a few minutes the tanks and half-tracks and trucks were rumbling out of Manila, headed north.

A dozen miles from Manila, part of the 194th turned to the left on Route 3 to approach the Agno River through Tarlac. To prevent the battalion from bogging down or being strafed as one large convoy, Colonel Miller sent Company A, my company, to the right on Route 5 toward Cabanatuan and San José. We maintained strict spacing between tanks and jounced along without incident until just south of San José. There we heard bombs ahead of us and then the rapid sharp sound of strafing planes. We could see the planes as they made their last passes and turned away toward the north.

My platoon entered the town a few minutes later. We learned that the people in San José had thought the planes were American. They had been out in the street waving excitedly, and the Zeros had strafed right down the main street. Houses had been blown apart on both sides of the road. We had to pick our way through debris and the bodies of men, women, and children. Here and there, shocked Filipinos were carrying the wounded to shelter. We were ordered to keep going. The platoon ahead of mine had been in the town when the attack came, and not one of them had been hit. This incident shocked us and brought the war home to us, even more than the attacks at Clark Field. Here the victims were defenseless civilians.

Our vehicles rumbled north through the late afternoon, turned west at the Agno River, and in the early evening arrived at our rendezvous point just south of the river at the small town of Carmen, where the main street ran north to a large bridge across the Agno. The commanders of Company A and Company D extricated us from the town, crowded with Philippine soldiers, and guided us into positions on the curving south bank of the river. We were strung out to cover a front of about 25 miles. As darkness fell, Lieutenant Hook, our platoon leader, spaced our tanks four or five yards apart facing the river. We were told that Philippine army units would join us as observers in front of the tanks, but we remained alone, facing the river in an area we had never scouted. Darkness settled on the dirt road leading back toward Carmen.

It was Christmas Eve, 1941.

3

THEY SHALL NOT PASS

WE WERE LESS than a mile from Carmen, and occasionally we could hear the Filipino soldiers singing "Silent Night" and "Adeste Fideles" in the distance. Each tank platoon had one man on guard while the others rested. For a long time we listened by the wide, placid river in the jungle growth, faintly hearing the Christmas songs from the town and listening for sounds of the Japanese army, which would soon try to cross the river.

The next morning, Christmas Day, was sunny and clear. The dry season was well under way. The river flowed slowly and muddily along in front of us. Occasionally, a Filipino farmer with a carabao cart would pass along the dirt road behind us. We worked on the tanks, tightening tracks and checking guns. Nothing happened. Faraway shelling reached our ears faintly.

About noon some trucks came up the road from Carmen. Sergeant Tex Simmons and Bill Kinler, from the battalion mess crew, yelled Christmas greetings and passed down hot Christmas dinners. They had cooked in Tarlac and tracked us down to deliver our last full Christmas dinner for a long, long time. We settled down after eating and waited again. Nothing happened for the rest of the afternoon and evening, despite the intermittent sounds of distant guns. We heard that some of the 26th Cavalry had passed through—badly shot up.

By the next morning I was nervous and restless. At my request Captain Burke gave me permission to walk into Carmen and look around. So I walked along the peaceful road with its high walls of jungle foliage and an occasional glimpse of the Agno River. The town was deserted except for small groups of Philippine soldiers. They were very young, with "coconut" hats. They held their rifles awkwardly, and many of them had no shoes. Some had chickens slung over their shoulders. But they were cheerful and waved and smiled at me. That

21

was the first time I saw and heard the greeting that became familiar later: the V sign and "Victory, Joe."

In the botica, or drugstore, the Filipino proprietor asked me if I thought the Japanese would cross the river and take the town. I said, "Well, I really don't know."

He poured me half a canteen cup of gin with some lemon flavoring, and that made me pretty strong. When he asked me a second time if the Japanese would cross the river and take the town, I said, "I don't think so."

It was then about 9:30 A.M., and we chatted some more, and he poured me another drink. As I started back to my platoon, he asked again if the Japanese would cross the river and take the town. I was very brave by then and replied like General Pétain at Verdun, "Ils ne passeront pas." ("They shall not pass.")

As soon as I got back to the tank crew, I heard the Japanese artillery opening up across the river and then heard the shells raining down on Carmen. The smoke from the town rose over the trees. Perhaps I should have told the Filipino in the botica that the odds were overwhelming that the Japanese would take the town.

4

RATTRAP ON THE AGNO RIVER

ABOUT HALF AN HOUR later on that clear blue morning, the Japanese artillery and mortars fired in earnest along the far bank of the river. A battery of our self-propelled mobile artillery replied. Each gun, a 75-millimeter piece, was mounted on a half-track, which would dart between two of our tanks, fire several rounds, and then pull back and go to a new position. The Japanese mortars would respond almost immediately, and we would button up our tanks. Lieutenant Hook would come down from the turret and pull the turret cover down. We were very crowded, and it was dark inside. As soon as the mortars stopped firing, we would move the tanks to a different position so that the Japanese heavy artillery, their 105-millimeter guns, wouldn't get us. Kenny Gordon, our driver, and Jim Bogart, our machine gunner and assistant driver, had slits to look out, but for the most part we were flying blind.

The firing gradually became heavier on both sides. The Japanese were trying to find places to ford the river, across sandbars and the shallow places, and also to set up gun positions clear of the heavy trees on the far bank. Our tanks were able to fire machine guns and 37-millimeter guns. The big gun on our tank was fired by Lieutenant Hook, the tank commander. This 37-millimeter shell could pierce armor, but it was not high-explosive, so it was mainly effective against armored vehicles rather than against infantry. For a while the Japanese troops took a severe beating. But as they brought up more artillery and stayed in the thick cover on the north bank, there was less for us to shoot at. One of our ammunition supply trucks was hit. In mid-afternoon two of the assistant drivers, Private Gerald Bell and Private August Bender, took the antiaircraft machine guns from two tank turrets and moved down to the river's edge to find a cleaner field of fire. We didn't see them again.

About the same time Sergeant Herbert Strobel had moved his tank into a new position, directing it from the open turret, and a lone round from one of the Japanese mortars hit a tree and exploded directly above the turret. Strobel was hit very badly, and his driver took a piece of shrapnel through his foot. A branch from the tree hit Colonel Miller on the head and knocked him down, but he got up and helped lift Strobel out of the tank and into a truck, which took Strobel, his driver, and some other wounded men out to an aid station. Strobel died that afternoon. This duel across the wide river went on until dark, and then our self-propelled mobile artillery left.

Colonel Miller had been worried about being caught in a rattrap if we were cut off from Route 3 through Carmen. The dirt road to the west of us crossed the river to the north bank, a crossing impassable for us. On the south bank, jungle and unexplored trails lay between us and Bayambang, where Route 13, the only good road west of us, ran south. One platoon of Company D, five tanks and five half-tracks, were supposed to be guarding that area, but we had no communication with them.

So before daylight died away completely, our company commander, Captain Burke, cautiously drove the only remaining jeep toward Carmen. A little way from the town, he continued on foot to scout what had happened and find us a route from our positions on the river. As he was working his way along the edge of the road, a machine gun fired on him. He was severely wounded and lay in a ditch beside the road until the next morning, when he was found by Japanese infantry troops. The Japanese officer in command was so impressed by Captain Burke's defiance that he ordered his soldiers not to harm him. Captain Burke was taken to a field hospital.

As soon as the Japanese machine gun opened fire on Captain Burke, Lieutenant Harold Costigan, in command of the nearest platoon of Company A, ordered his tanks to return the fire. It immediately became clear that the Japanese were in Carmen in force. Lieutenant Costigan got his platoon together, and his four or five tanks—at top speed and firing every gun they had—went down the road right in the teeth of the Japanese fire. They slammed through a probably incomplete Japanese roadblock and drove into town and turned south on Route 3 in a rain of fire. One tank missed the corner and blazed through the intersection down the road three miles to Rosales, where he could turn south on another road, which he had all to himself.

Lieutenant Costigan's group kept firing all the way out of Carmen. In the darkness a Japanese soldier tossed a thermite bomb on the flat deck of one of the tanks. It burned through the iron plate and dropped into the main ammunition tray. Luckily, all four crew members got out as the tank went up in flames, and they were picked up by the following tank.

But back at the river we knew only that firing had broken out, our company commander hadn't returned, and some tanks had charged into an inferno of firing. Then all was quiet, and we waited in the darkness. We had no way of knowing that the 192nd Tank Battalion had pulled out, along with most of one Philippine army outfit, and that the Japanese had crossed the Agno River about 1,000 yards the other side of Carmen and had quickly overpowered the resistance of the remaining infantry. We were flanked and bottled up in our rattrap west of Carmen.

We waited all night. It was still quiet in the morning. I heard a rooster crowing near Carmen. About mid-morning Captain Jack Altman, the commander of Company D, came from his position west of us. He got together a group of men from our Company A. He told us that he had tried to raise battalion headquarters and tank-group headquarters on the radio, but all the radio signals were jammed. All he could get was static. We could tell that he felt something was very wrong. He had already learned that Captain Burke hadn't come back from his scouting excursion.

Captain Altman sent a half-track, commanded by Lieutenant John Hummel, down the road toward Carmen. We heard firing after a few minutes. The half-track came back toward us and stopped in the middle of the road. The crew piled out, grabbed the guns, and ran toward us up the road. Lieutenant Hummel had been shot through the neck, and he held his fingers over the entry and exit wounds until he could get medical help.

At this point in our uncertainty and confusion, Captain Altman took command of the seven remaining tanks of Company A as well as his own tank crews in Company D. He did not issue hard and fast orders, but he said we should head south across some cane fields to a carabao-cart trail that he hoped would parallel Route 3, so we might get ahead of the Japanese and rejoin our own battalion. He made it clear to us that we might be lucky and we might not be. One Company A tank commander decided that he and his crew would try to get away from the encircling Japanese by heading farther west. Eventually, they joined the guerrillas in an area near Clark Field and Fort Stotsenburg.

The rest of us, trusting in Captain Altman's good sense, went single file through the fields, jolting up and over the low earth banks between fields, until we found the carabao-cart trail and made our way south. About nine tanks from Company D made up the rest of the column. The half-track crew, including the wounded Lieutenant Hummel, were allotted places in various tanks along with a few other wounded. We found a tiny Filipino barrio, or village, but no one could tell us anything about the Japanese army or even the best way back to Route 3. We paralleled the railroad embankment for a while and finally edged onto Route 3 a short distance north of Moncada. We opened up the tanks and headed for the bridge across the river at Moncada. About 30 minutes before sunset we reached the thoroughly demolished bridge. The railway bridge was also a shambles. We had no way to get our tanks across.

On the chance that we could come back and retrieve the tanks, Captain Altman ordered us to remove parts from the engines and hide them in thick jungle, to prevent the Japanese from salvaging the tanks. Darkness had fallen by the time we left the 15 tanks and began to cross the river, partly swimming and partly crawling on the fallen bridge girders. Men who could swim especially well towed the wounded across. I wasn't wounded, but I couldn't swim. I borrowed three canteens and emptied them, and with my own canteen they served as a life preserver. In the stress of the moment I got myself across the river.

When we were all on the other side, Captain Altman sent a group down the road toward Tarlac for help. They found some guards in a jeep on outpost duty. Battalion headquarters soon sent some trucks to pick us up. We were cold and wet when we climbed stiffly out of the trucks near Tarlac.

Phil Brain, with a tommy gun under his arm, brought me a blanket. "I thought you were lost," he said. Phil, a fellow draftee from Minnesota, was a close friend of mine.

"I got news for you," I said. "I thought we were lost too."

Late at night as it was, we got a mess kit full of hot stew and coffee, and we were issued K rations, in case we had to move again unexpectedly. Whenever possible, Colonel Miller made sure we were fed well. He kept the men with field kitchens almost always on semi-standby. I ate and rolled up in a blanket under some acacia trees.

5

GUARDING THE CALUMPIT BRIDGES

*T*HE NEXT DAY we licked our wounds, serviced our remaining tanks, cleaned and oiled guns, and caught up on sleep under the trees. We heard how Colonel Miller, with three tanks and one of the self-propelled mobile artillery commanded by Lieutenant Gordon Peck, had decisively turned back the Japanese at San Manuel, a few miles south of Carmen. That roadblock had ambushed the Japanese column so thoroughly that the Japanese retreated to Carmen and set up defensive positions, expecting a counterattack.

Late in that afternoon of December 29 I awoke to find the area astir. The orders were to move out at dusk to the Calumpit bridges again. This time there was a bright moon, and driving was easier and safer. The roads were still choked with refugees. At daylight the next morning we reached our new bivouac area, strung out from the west end of the bridges back up the road to Apalit, two miles to the northwest where Colonel Miller set up headquarters. I was reassigned to a new tank, with Kenny Gordon again as the driver, and we were put in position to repel any Japanese attempt to take either the highway bridge or the railway bridge at Calumpit. We also were to make certain that no one prematurely blew up the bridges, which had been heavily mined by Colonel Harry K. Skerry and his engineers.

These two crucial bridges, over the Pampanga River north of Manila Bay, had to be held for our South Luzon Force, which was executing a delaying action against the Japanese forces that had invaded the long Bicol Peninsula, to the southeast of Manila. Manila was to be abandoned to this Japanese pincer movement from north and south, after all the Philippine and American forces had withdrawn into the Bataan Peninsula, where, in conjunction with the island of Corregidor,

27

we would control the entrance to Manila Bay. Meanwhile, our South
Luzon Force would be trapped and destroyed if we didn't hold the
Calumpit bridges for those troops to withdraw northwest through
Manila, across the bridges to San Fernando, and around the bay south
into Bataan. As soon as our forces were across, we'd blow the bridges.
So we guarded the bridges and watched the traffic, military and civilian
vehicles almost bumper to bumper on their way to the Bataan Peninsula. For some time we had been confident, because we had been
repeatedly told that Bataan was a fortress of prepared positions with
ample supplies.

During the next 48 hours, December 30 and 31, the traffic never
ceased. Refugees went by on foot, in carabao carts, and in the horse-
drawn carriages called calesas. Small children rode on the slow
carabao. Pambuscos, or buses, and passenger cars were filled with
civilians evacuating Manila. I was sure that Bataan was well provisioned
because so many of the vehicles, particularly the military trucks, carried no supplies. Then, on one of his many inspections of the chaos
of traffic at the highway bridge, Colonel Miller stopped to talk to
another tank-crew member, pointing at a line of military trucks, and
said, "Hell! They're empty!" I felt a sinking sensation.

Colonel Miller began to count the empty trucks, and then he
ordered Major Canby, his executive officer, to assemble a detail of
trucks and set out to salvage gasoline and canned goods from the abandoned depots on the highway north of us. He even sent one group all
the way to Fort Stotsenburg. Lieutenant Ralph Duby, the young
recreation officer, was so overwhelmed by what had been left behind
at Fort Stotsenburg that he brought back a complete set of military
china—causing groans and laughter for months. But Colonel Miller
managed to send into Bataan, to a guarded supply dump near Orion,
12,000 gallons of high-octane gasoline and 6 truckloads of canned food.

On December 31 there was a persistent rumor that the next day
we would go on half rations. The order, soon made official, came from
General MacArthur himself. Meanwhile, we made the best of the two
hot meals a day from our field kitchens.

As during our earlier stay at Calumpit, we watched the sky and
waited for the Japanese air force to blast the area and destroy the mined
bridges, but during our two days in position at Calumpit, they made
only occasional and half-hearted attempts to bomb us. We had an antiaircraft detachment of the 200th Coast Artillery, but the glide-and-

bomb attacks were driven off with few hits. Perhaps three planes went off trailing smoke. They showed none of the polished accuracy that the Japanese navy fliers had displayed at Clark Field in the first week of the war. They didn't strafe the road. They could have fatally blocked the traffic to Bataan. The days were bright with sunshine, and the dust clouds and glints of reflected light from windshields and headlights must have made a perfect target. Later they bombed and strafed in earnest, but we were well into Bataan by then.

6

INTO BATAAN

W E BEGAN EVACUATING our positions at the Calumpit bridges just before midnight on December 31. The last tanks of the 192nd, scarred by a wild, bitter fight at Plaridel, a few miles east of the bridges, rumbled across the highway bridge at about 2:30 on that morning of January 1, 1942. When we left, we knew that the bridges might be blown at any time, and on our way northwest to our new defensive positions near San Fernando, we heard a distant explosion above the racket of our tanks. The long triple-span steel and concrete bridges had gone up, with the wide Pampanga River between us and the Japanese forces to the east. At daylight we were at the outskirts of San Fernando.

Men called "Happy New Year," but for me the spirit was missing. I, and others, had a feeling of foreboding. San Fernando was like a ghost town, a far cry from the busy commercial center and provincial capital that we had come to on weekend passes before the war. Now, from San Fernando south, the 194th Tank Battalion with elements of the 192nd would provide the main covering force for a rearguard action so that other units could reach Bataan and assume a unified defensive position.

On that New Year's Day there was a sharp clash at our outpost at Mexico, a few miles north and east of San Fernando. Late that night the last Philippine troops moved south across the bridge over the San Fernando River. At about 2:00 A.M. the last of the 194th tanks rolled across, and the bridge was blown. We were now on Route 7, the main road into Bataan through Guagua, Lubao, Remedios, and Santa Crus to Layac Junction, about 25 miles south of San Fernando.

Our first delaying position was at Guagua, the southeast end of a tenuous line from Porac to Guagua, at the edge of the swamps along the head of Pampanga Bay, the north arm of Manila Bay. A small, dusty road joined the two towns. At the southern edge of Guagua a bridge gave access to a muddy byroad that went south, parallel to Route 7, to Sexmoan and then turned to rejoin Route 7 a few miles to our rear. We destroyed this bridge and established an outpost at Betis, a short way back toward San Fernando. We passed a day without being attacked. Colonel Miller set up a roadblock at the far end of the byroad through Sexmoan, in case the Japanese got around and onto that muddy road, and another roadblock on the road to Floridablanca, a small town to the west of us. We were not to be trapped without a back door again.

On January 3 the outpost at Betis, a platoon of tanks from Company C, was driven back into Guagua, and late in the day the Japanese artillery began to register on the town. By the next afternoon the artillery was coupled with intense mortar fire but little bombing and strafing. Lubao, the next town on the way southwest to Layac Junction, was almost obliterated by air attack. At daylight on January 5 the enemy fire of all kinds made the Guagua-Porac line untenable. We were ordered to withdraw. Again the 194th Tank Battalion would cover the withdrawal and be the last troops out, and as usual there were mixups and confusion. Somehow we made it out of Guagua—battered but still intact.

Colonel Miller's caution in establishing the roadblocks behind us was almost nullified when General Weaver ordered both outpost units away from the roadblocks and sent them on into Bataan with the medical personnel of the 194th and the 192nd. Luckily, Colonel Miller, as was his habit, sent his executive officer, Captain Spoor, to check on them. Spoor found both outposts gone, and Miller sent units back to replace them, just in time. As soon as the roadblock on the Sexmoan road had been reestablished, down that muddy byroad from Guagua and Sexmoan came 500 Japanese infantry with light artillery in support. The roadblock became an ambush, and the Japanese column was nearly destroyed, with its remnants retreating toward Guagua.

So we retreated down Route 7 through Lubao, which had been badly bombed earlier. At the barrio of Remedios we halted for the night. Trucks from the rear echelon brought in a hot meal. Half-track outposts went into position, and we prepared to spend the night alternating sleep with sentry duty. It was a long day, that January 5.

Sometime after midnight I awoke with a start. There was firing from several directions. Kenny Gordon yelled, "Take cover! and we piled into the tank. The sentries had warned us in time. After two hours we drove off the attack. The Japanese lost men, and we had a number of wounded, including the man who did the most to organize this defense: Lieutenant Petrie, who died from his wounds a week later. He was awarded the Distinguished Service Cross posthumously.

This "fire and fall back" action was typical of the covering job of the 194th Tank Battalion. The positions after San Fernando became blurred in my mind. The land was flat and dusty, and the trees and barrios looked much the same. We held a position and fired, and when night came, we fell back to another position. We acted mechanically in a punch-drunk condition. As we passed out of the rice-growing area south of San Fernando and as the cover near the road became scarcer, we feared air attack. Finally, on January 7 we were told to pass through our defending lines to a rear bivouac area for rest and servicing of all vehicles — tanks, trucks, and half-tracks. The 194th was the last unit to enter Bataan.

Unfortunately, the bivouac area selected by General Weaver turned out to be only 500 yards behind the front lines, and almost immediately Japanese artillery began to register uncomfortably close. Colonel Miller went through the tiresome business of requesting to move out of artillery range. Then all troops withdrew to the defensive position known as the Abucay Hacienda line.

We settled into a new bivouac area and our first real breathing spell since December 24. But our spirits dropped when we looked around. We had been told that Bataan was fortified and impregnable, but all we saw were some partially dug foxholes in front of the main area of resistance on the Abucay Hacienda line. Our new bivouac area was well chosen, though. Jungle trees and heavy undergrowth gave good protection from air attack. We were on a slight rise off the main road to the southern tip of Bataan, with Pampanga Bay in sight to the east of us. We set up an outpost near the beach to guard against a Japanese landing.

7

THE FIRST LINE

NOW BEHIND the Abucay Hacienda line, we began servicing and repairing our vehicles in earnest—and also improvising. Spare parts were almost as scarce as food. In the jungle of prewar red tape the port-area quartermaster in Manila had repeatedly refused to release our supplies of maintenance equipment, as day by day the last moments of peace had ticked away.

We began to have a clear idea of the corner we had backed into. The peninsula of Bataan is 30 miles long from north to south and about 14 miles from east to west at the widest point. The China Sea and Subic Bay lie on the west side, and Manila Bay lies on the east. Down the middle rises a chain of extinct volcanoes: Mount Santa Rosa, Mount Natib, Mount Silanganan, Mount Samat, Mount Bataan, and the Mariveles Mountains toward the tip of the peninsula. The mountainous area is rough, rising abruptly from the narrow coastal strip to heights of nearly 5,000 feet. Most of this area is covered with heavy jungle renewed each year in the wet season, which usually lasts from June into November. Now it was dry and hot. Everywhere empty water courses led out of the mountains.

Had Bataan been provisioned and had fortifications been built in advance, many months and many more Japanese divisions would have been required to take Bataan. The terrain made a formidable obstacle. The chief reason for defending Bataan was that until Bataan was taken, the Japanese could not attack Corregidor and the smaller islands stretching from the tip of Bataan across the entrance to Manila Bay: Corregidor (Fort Mills), Caballo (Fort Hughes), El Fraile (Fort Drum), and Carabao (Fort Frank). The important harbor of Manila Bay was denied to the Japanese navy and to Japanese shipping. And our resistance was a festering thorn to the Japanese military pride.

Communications between the two sides of the Bataan Peninsula

33

were difficult, so each side became a separate command. The I Corps area on the China Sea side to the west was commanded by General Jonathan M. Wainwright, and the II Corps area on the Manila Bay side was commanded by General George M. Parker. The 194th Tank Battalion was assigned to General Parker, to be held as reserve and as beach defense. We were often called upon to stop breaks in the lines—sometimes in places where tanks could not be driven.

For two weeks in the middle of January the Japanese hurled wave after wave of infantry at the Abucay Hacienda line, especially against the II Corps under General Parker. And night after night we saw trucks, ambulances, and converted pambuscos with makeshift bunks, bringing the wounded past our bivouac area to the two field hospitals near the town of Mariveles near the southern tip of Bataan. Dust from the road drifted over us as the vehicles jounced cautiously down toward the hospitals.

During part of this period I was assigned to duty with the battalion radio on the communications half-track. Occasionally, we were allowed the luxury of tuning in to station KGEI of San Francisco. Usually, off-duty soldiers gathered around the half-track to listen. One evening the announcer from San Francisco gave a graphic description of the blackout of the U.S. west coast and warned of the danger of Japanese invasion. Sergeant Major Bill Boyd broke in with his quiet Texan drawl: "Call them back and tell them to hold out for 30 days and we'll give them a hand." The announcer also went into great detail about MacArthur roaming the Bataan front lines and encouraging the troops. We listened to that with stony amusement. MacArthur made only one trip to Bataan from his headquarters on Corregidor: on January 10 he stopped briefly at General Parker's and General Wainwright's respective headquarters. There had been a hasty summoning of all unit commanders to be present.

On another night, during some of the heaviest fighting when the roads were full of the ambulances and pambuscos taking casualties to the field hospital, the same announcer said dramatically, "All the United States mourns the death of Carole Lombard in an airplane crash." He ended by saying, "Our losses on Bataan are relatively light."

During this time the Japanese soldiers proved themselves well trained at infiltration. They concealed themselves in trees and waited to pick off American officers, particularly those assigned to the Philippine army. These snipers were so effective that soon the officers removed their insignia. Another trick was to infiltrate and set off strings of firecrackers behind our lines. This was demoralizing, especially on the newly inducted and only partially trained Philippine army units.

We had our own methods of relieving our frustration. For instance, on outpost duty we had a half-track commanded by Sergeant Sid Saign. The crew would carefully take up a concealed position at the edge of a clearing. One man with a white cloth fastened to a stick would wait for the Japanese reconnaissance plane known to us as Photo Joe. When the plane got near, the man would wave the white cloth on the stick. Photo Joe would glide in to investigate, and if he came within range, Sid Saign would open up with a 50-caliber machine gun. Sometimes Photo Joe left smoking, and everyone on the half-track would give a cheer.

The position on the Abucay Hacienda line changed several times. Whenever there was a halt in the fighting, the dead were buried where they fell. More often, they had to be left behind. We knew how serious the situation was when our 31st Infantry, bivouacked near us, was alerted to prevent the Japanese from breaking through. The 31st and the 45th and 57th Philippine Scouts were the backbone of the reserve force, the best-trained and best-armed infantry regiments on Bataan.

Amidst the chaos of the crumbling of the Abucay Hacienda line, many soldiers were separated from their units. Some were killed, and some managed to work their way back to the new Filipino-American positions later. Often the help of Filipinos saved them. One such soldier was Sergeant Burt Ellis. On the morning of January 20, when Company I of the 31st Infantry attacked to recover lost ground, Burt was shot in both legs halfway across a dry rice paddy. For a long time he lay there, bleeding and stunned, vaguely aware of the fighting going on around him. Late in the afternoon the Japanese counterattacked in force and swept back across the rice paddy. Charging past, a Japanese soldier bayoneted Burt twice, once in the stomach and once in the side.

That night, after the attack had been carried on to the south, a brave Filipino doctor came with a lantern to see who might be living. He would have been shot if a Japanese patrol had spotted him. The doctor got Burt onto an improvised litter and had him carried to the small church at Abucay. Burt was bandaged and was given a blood transfusion through a rubber tube directly from a Filipino nurse. Burt passed the next few days and nights in a blur of semiconsciousness. He knew dimly that the doctor had found people to hide him. On the night of January 26 he was laid on the bottom of a carabao cart and covered with a huge pile of rice straw. He was carried on trails through the Japanese lines and the American lines to the field hospital near Little Baquio. Burt began to recover there and later, as a war prisoner, in Bilibid Prison. Eventually he was sent to Cabanatuan Prison Camp.

8

WITHDRAWAL

D AY AFTER DAY the fighting continued. The Japanese were unable to make headway against the well-defended positions on the west, from Mauban inland, or against the more heavily defended position at the east end of the line, inland from Mabatang, just north of Abucay. But we could not protect or even patrol the rugged mountains around Mount Santa Rosa, Mount Natib, and Mount Silanganan, between the I Corps on the west and the II Corps on the east. By about January 20 the Japanese had shifted enough troops to exploit this basic weakness of the Abucay Hacienda line. They threatened to turn the inland flanks of both corps. But our long hold on the Abucay Hacienda line had given us time to prepare new positions on an all-weather gravel road across the waist of Bataan, so on January 24 we began a withdrawal eight miles south to this new line, called the Pilar-Bagac line.

The 194th Battalion was ordered north to cover the withdrawal, as the rear echelon was ordered south. One of the truck drivers with the rear echelon was a fellow draftee from Minnesota, Harry Heikkila. He and Andy Kelly, another Minnesotan, who was riding shotgun, somehow got ahead of the group and drove south past the new bivouac area near Lamao. Eventually, they stopped to ask directions at the quartermaster food depot near Mariveles. Harry got out of the truck to speak to a nattily dressed young lieutenant.

Before Harry opened his mouth, the lieutenant said, "Don't you know enough to salute an officer?" "I didn't know I was that far back, sir," Harry replied, peeling off a rigid salute. Harry and Andy kept their faces straight while they turned the truck around to head back north to the new bivouac area.

The combat elements of the 194th went north on a rough track known as the Back Road. This brushed out and bladed track ran north

37

and south parallel to the main east road, Route 110, and about two and a half miles to the west of it. Like most of the so-called roads the engineers made on Bataan, it had been built hastily with back-breaking labor. It was about 20 feet wide. The surface was hard and dusty, but beside the road was an unsafe crust of dried vegetation. The jungle was a wall on either side. The road twisted around huge mahogany and banyan trees, and a tank that was not surely handled could become mired 10 feet off the edge of a turn. The gullies and streambeds had to be bridged, even in the dry season. The Back Road was a nightmare to drive on after dark, and in the daytime the dust rose out of the jungle as a tell-tale signal to Japanese strafing planes. By the late afternoon of January 24 the 194th was in its assigned place at the northernmost point of the Back Road, where it made a T junction with the Abucay Hacienda line.

The withdrawal began as scheduled, but by the time the hard-pressed units reached this intersection, they had become a milling herd, and there were no guides or military police to direct them. Units became hopelessly enmeshed with other units. Men who were separated from their officers moved any way that took them away from the pursuing Japanese. Officers from the covering force, such as Colonel Miller, helped move the mass along. Then the Japanese launched an attack from the west against the left flank of our line. Luckily, this flank was held by the rear guard of the American 31st and the 45th Philippine Scout Infantry. Had the Japanese attacked directly at the center, where we were, or had they interdicted the T junction with artillery, there would have been a slaughter and a rout, and they could probably have marched to the tip of Bataan. But the crisis passed.

The left flank sustained a heavy attack. Some of the 194th, with an attached battery of self-propelled mobile artillery, moved to the left and supported the infantry companies of the 31st and 45th. They were then able to retreat through us. Many were wounded, and they all were dog tired and starving. One first sergeant walked over to where our tanks were in position and said, "I'm McNulty, First Sergeant of Company L, 31st Infantry. Thanks!" He stumbled off to a pambusco to be jolted down the Back Road to the rear. A few months later he was in charge of our barracks in Cabanatuan Prison Camp.

Just before daylight the 194th received orders to pull back south a short way to an east-west trail known as the Cadre Road, very narrow and hemmed in by heavy jungle. There were no American or Filipino forces to the north of us. Uneasily, we made the best of it and established ourselves in this cramped and almost indefensible position. On the next evening we received the correct orders to pull farther to the south behind the outpost line near the Banibani Road, so that we could cover the further withdrawal. The Banibani Road was an east-west track that led from Route 110 on Manila Bay across the Back Road and then meandered west and south until it joined the Pilar-Bagac road.

By about 1:00 A.M. all the units we were covering had moved past us toward the new line of defense. We could hardly see them in the dark, but we could hear them and feel them. Then we started to leave. A short distance down the rough trail we came to a narrow bridge. The tank I was in ran partly off the edge of the bridge and became stuck. We piled out of the tank as it teetered on the edge and, working awkwardly in the dark and dusty night, we tried to pull it back onto the bridge with cables. The tank fell off the bridge and landed upside down in the streambed under the bridge. Under pressure of time, the commander of Company A reported to Colonel Miller, who told him to destroy the tank and continue the withdrawal. A 37-millimeter shell from one of the other tanks set the derelict on fire. The burning gasoline showed us the low, sluggish waters of the stream, and we got the last few vehicles over the bridge and continued south.

Then a tank from one of the other companies ran off the road and tipped onto its side. We sweated blood futilely trying to retrieve it. Colonel Miller radioed our predicament to General Weaver. Colonel Miller became exasperated in requesting a tank wrecker to be sent up from the rear. We could hear the general's voice insistently repeating, "Bring out all Chesterfields" (the code name for the tanks). It was almost daylight, and we had no supporting infantry. All the Filipino-American forces were to the south, and the Japanese were to the west and north of us and were closing fast.

While the ridiculous and infuriating battle with headquarters went on, Colonel Miller put the tanks and the half-tracks into the best defensive positions possible. We were strung out along the Back Road, the north-south trail we must retreat along, at the intersection with the Banibani Road. Outposts were sent to watch for trouble to the north and to the west. Miller organized the artillery battery on a knoll just behind us to the east of the Back Road. We were still more than two miles north of the main defensive position at the Pilar-Bagac line.

From the half-track to which I had been assigned after the tank had gone off the bridge, I heard one of our outposts call out a challenge and start firing. A Japanese patrol was coming on the Banibani Road from the west. Immediately, machine-gun and mortar fire from the west came at us all along our column. The tanks and half-tracks opened up with all their guns, and the Japanese artillery zeroed in on the jungle growth and treetops just behind us. Suddenly there seemed to be Japanese everywhere, and they all seemed to have mortars.

Above the din of the firing, some nearby Philippine Scouts were yelling in cadence as they loaded their artillery, "Tojo, count your men." And after they had fired the shell, they yelled, "Tojo, *now* count your men." They were cool, tough soldiers, those Philippine Scouts.

Toward noon the Japanese planes circled overhead, apparently uncertain about the position of their own troops. Then from the north the Japanese artillery began to register uncomfortably close to us. Colonel Miller ordered the column to retreat slowly to the south down the Back Road, still firing machine guns as we went. By early afternoon we had passed through the Filipino-American lines. Men were still hard at work on defensive positions. Unknown to us, the Japanese, expecting to split our forces by landing on the west coast just north of the town of Mariveles, intended to drive a wedge into the new Pilar-Bagac line before our troops could dig in. Our chance battle on the morning of January 26 blunted their drive, and they were forced to reorganize north of the Pilar-Bagac road.

9

THE SECOND LINE

AFTER A FEW DAYS of settling into our bivouac area near
Lamao, the various units of the 194th were assigned specific
duties. Some went on beach defense near the small town of Cabcaben
to the south of us and at Limay landing, the larger town about two
miles north of us and less than two miles from the end of the front line
on Manila Bay. Others were on standby reserve in case of a major
assault by the Japanese against the Pilar-Bagac line.

Because of the demonstrated superiority of the communication
section of the 194th Tank Battalion since December 8, II Corps headquarters ordered the battalion to establish a radio centrale (pronounced
as if the second word were Spanish) to correlate ground radio and our
navy patrol boats operating in Manila Bay. This radio centrale also
handled all communications for tank-group headquarters in keeping
track of the 192nd Tank Battalion, the 194th, and the 17th Ordnance
Company.

I spent most of my time assigned to our radio centrale. Six tankers
manned the centrale, two hours on and four hours off, 24 hours a day.
Set up in an old commercial panel truck which we had salvaged during
the withdrawal into Bataan, we were concealed on a heavily wooded
knoll on the eastern edge of the battalion area, where we had a fine
view of Manila Bay.

A short time before our withdrawal from the Abucay Hacienda
line to the Pilar-Bagac line, General Homma requested General Naoki
Kimura, the Japanese commander on the west side of Bataan, to in-
itiate landings behind the American lines. Homma was impressed by
General Tomoyuki Yamashita's success with amphibious landings
against the British in Malaya. Kimura committed two battalions of the
Japanese 20th Infantry Division to four landings from the west, on the
China Sea. One landing, at Longoskawayan Point, was only 3,000

yards from Mariveles, opposite Corregidor. Because the Pilar-Bagac line was holding, the crack Philippine Scout troops of the 57th and 45th Scout regiments, accompanied by tanks from the 192nd Battalion, could be released to contain and destroy these Japanese landings in close-quarter jungle fighting. Only a few Japanese escaped, picked up by their landing barges at night and taken back to Olongapo. The two battalions of the Japanese 20th Infantry were finished. But the Scouts paid heavily too: some companies suffered 50 percent casualties. Had General Kimura been able to reinforce these landings, Bataan would have been cut off from Corregidor and so it would have fallen much sooner.

At the same time as these landings on the China Sea side of Bataan, the Japanese made an all-out effort to cut through the Pilar-Bagac line in the middle of the I Corps area. These attackers were encircled and entrapped in what became known as the Battle of the Big and Little Pockets. The Little Pocket was wiped out first. The Japanese drove a salient into the Pilar-Bagac line to save the Big Pocket, but it too was destroyed in some of the most difficult fighting in Bataan. One company of wounded and starving Japanese soldiers found a gap at the north of the closing circle. Traveling at night, having buried most of their equipment, they escaped back to their own lines.

On February 10 the Japanese 14th Army, exhausted as an attacking force, withdrew into defensive positions north of the Pilar-Bagac line. General Homma called a meeting of his staff at San Fernando to consider his awkward situation. As was common procedure with all Japanese armies, the majors and colonels of the army's operation section—the real power of any Japanese army—reviewed the 14th Army's predicament and debated what should be done. General Homma, according to Japanese custom, was present but did not participate in the discussion. The decision of the staff was to suspend operations against the Filipino-American forces and to ask for reinforcements from Japan. This meant public disgrace for General Homma. As the meeting ended, Homma fainted. He was carried out of the meeting.

The Japanese 14th Army's request for reinforcements had two serious consequences: Colonel Tokushiro Hattori, of operations headquarters in Tokyo, designed the final attack on the Pilar-Bagac line himself, and for reinforcements he sent Colonel Masanobu Tsuji, one of the most fanatical and powerful officers in the Japanese army. Colonel

Tsuji had committed atrocities in Singapore. He wished to exterminate not only the Americans but also the Filipinos who, he felt, had betrayed the Asiatic world by helping the Americans.

After the elimination of the landings on the west coast of Bataan and the destruction of the pockets on the Pilar-Bagac line, we fought enemies more formidable than the Japanese: hunger and disease. It was a battle that could not be won. Malaria and dysentery were the earliest and most obviously crippling diseases. The two field hospitals contained so many wounded soldiers that Colonel Miller ordered our battalion medical unit to set up a treatment center for our own sick. Litters served as beds, each protected by a mosquito bar. Miguel García, a Philippine Scout in the 26th Cavalry, and his Filipino helpers built more beds from bamboo. Dr. Leo Schneider, the senior medical officer of the 194th Tank Battalion, acquired powdered quinine and built a small machine to manufacture pills for those with malaria. I had my second attack of malaria in the second week of February. Immediately afterward I came down with dysentery, then scurvy, and then a sinus infection that to this day bothers me. Many of us, including me, became night blind.

Up to the middle of February I still had hope that somehow the combined Allied naval forces would reach us in time. The optimistic communiqué that MacArthur issued on January 15 had fanned our hope: "Help is on the way from the United States. Thousands of troops and hundreds of planes are being dispatched. The exact time of arrival of reinforcements is unknown, as they will have to fight their way through Japanese attempts against them. . . . Our supplies are ample." This morale-building rhetoric was falsely reinforced by another story, officially issued by USAFFE in a mimeographed newssheet. According to this article, a newspaper correspondent had accompanied, from the United States to Australia, a huge convoy bound for Bataan and Corregidor. When I heard of the fall of Singapore, the chief Allied fortress and naval base in the Far East, I knew there was no hope for us. I argued with more optimistic friends and pored over maps in the communications truck.

After my malaria attack and dysentery, I returned to duty at the radio centrale. The lull in the fighting continued. The Japanese were content to let us fight hunger and disease, and no large-scale Japanese attack was expected before April. Occasionally at night Japanese landing barges with one heavy artillery piece would sneak across the bay from Manila and shell the beaches near us. They always sheared off and ran at the first reply from our artillery. The beaches were well patrolled by our half-tracks and tanks. Late at night, when not on duty at the radio centrale, I would walk down to the beach and see the tropical moon and its path of warm light quivering on Manila Bay. Resting on the horizon to the south were the brilliant stars of the Southern Cross.

One of the best-trained of the communications men, Sergeant Jerry Lundquist, was my duty partner at the radio centrale. We had been drafted the same day and sent out together to Fort Lewis, Washington, to join the 194th Tank Battalion. Jerry was well educated, and he thoroughly enjoyed singing, as I did. We liked to listen to KGEI in San Francisco and to KZRH in Manila, under Japanese control then. Oddly enough, both stations played recordings of the "Battle Hymn of the Republic." Jerry and I would hum along, whiling away the hungry hours on duty.

In late February and the first few days of March rumors were rife that MacArthur was not only going to leave Corregidor for some unknown destination but that he was to leave by PT boat. So one evening about March 1, when Jerry and I were humming along with the "Battle Hymn of the Republic," we began to make up our own words—about MacArthur's part in the conditions on Bataan, his imminent departure, and our plight, unreinforced and starving.

USAFFE Cry of Freedom

Dugout Doug MacArthur lies ashaking on the Rock,
Safe from all the bombers and any sudden shock.
Dugout Doug is eating of the best food on Bataan,
And his troops go starving on.

Chorus:
Dugout Doug, come out from hiding,
Dugout Doug, come out from hiding,
Send to Franklin these glad tidings
That his troops go starving on!

Dugout Doug's not timid, he's just cautious, not afraid.
He's protecting carefully the stars that Franklin made.
Four-star generals are as rare as food is on Bataan,
And his troops go starving on.

Dugout Doug is ready in his Chris-Craft for the flee
Over the bounding billows and the wildly raging sea,
For the Japs are pounding on the gates of old Bataan,
And his troops go starving on.

We've fought the war the hard way since they said the fight was on,
All the way from Lingayen to the hills of old Bataan,
And we'll continue fighting after Dugout Doug is gone,
And still go starving on.

We sang out the improvised verses to the relief crew, and we all had a good laugh. Next morning we realized that this was not the end of our venture into versifying. One of the relief crew had written down the words, and Colonel Miller had found some men laughing over the song. At noon a runner came down from battalion headquarters to the radio centrale and told us that Colonel Miller wanted to know who had written the verses about MacArthur. Jerry and I foresaw an immediate court-martial. Fortunately, the runner had been chosen for fearlessness and speed, not for education or quickness of wit. With a nod from Jerry, I allowed that a Greek soldier by the name of Anonymous had visited us the evening before and had given us the verses in question. The runner returned to battalion headquarters. Jerry and I hoped the incident would end there, but other units picked up the song and added more verses.

By March 1, 1942, we defenders of Bataan were holding an area about 13 miles wide by 13 miles long. One day I saw my friend José Sanchez near Hospital Number One, and he shook his head and said, "As a gambler, I tell you we are double losers! Thirteen by thirteen." Here were crammed 78,000 Filipino and American soldiers and 20,000 Filipino and American refugees, many of whom worked in some capacity for the army. Even the most inaccurate bombing by the Japanese usually hit something or somebody.

But we had become so conditioned by hunger and disease that, except when he was sent on patrol, the average soldier paid little attention to the enemy. And when MacArthur left by PT boat for Australia on March 12, no one I met in the forward units expressed interest.

10

OF MALARIA AND IGUANAS

THE AVERAGE AMERICAN soldier's weight loss by the end of March was close to 30 pounds—in addition to the average of 10 pounds lost getting into Bataan. Because we had been split up into various units for beach defense, front-line reserve, and communications, I often did not see a good friend for two or three weeks. Then when we met, we were aware of the loose clothing, the thin faces, and the sunken eyes.

We came to realize that USAFFE had failed to provision Bataan with food and other supplies that had been available in the Philippines but had not been moved. The fuel in Manila had been destroyed at the last minute, although it could have previously been shipped across the bay to Bataan. In addition, 10 million tons of rice had not been moved from a depot at Cabanatuan, only 100 miles from Bataan. The navy and the few marines at Mariveles had been prepared with a tunnel with showers, clothes, and food sufficient for their number. Now they were ordered to share their supplies with the army. The navy men were generous with their food: any friend got a meal and a chance to shower and shave. But if the navy could be prepared, why not USAFFE?

As tankers, sometimes on the front lines and sometimes back at Lamao, we realized how desperate the food supply problem was for front-line outfits. Colonel Miller's six truckloads of food, picked up from the supply dumps at Fort Stotsenburg and elsewhere before we were locked into Bataan, were depleted after having been rationed to the sick during late February and early March.

Most of the men developed a caustic sense of humor. I remember running into Sergeant James Jones, who had come over to Manila on the same ship with us in September. His outfit, the 200th Antiaircraft, had protected us from planes on many occasions. One day he said with a straight face, "Did you hear about Wainwright calling MacArthur in Australia?" "No," I answered. "What did he say?" "He said, 'Douglas, my men are too weak to carry their rifles.'" I realized then it was a joke, and I said, "What did Douglas say to that?" Jones grinned. "Douglas said, 'Jonathan, issue the men pistols.'"

In spite of the hunger and disease, American instructors were teaching infantry tactics to the Philippine army just behind the front line. This training should have been given during the five prewar years of MacArthur's Philippine command. Later, in Cabanatuan Prison Camp, Major Karl Bahr, a West Point graduate, told me that he had never trained more capable and dedicated soldiers than the Philippine soldiers he trained behind the front lines between February 15 and April 1, 1942.

Our bivouac area near Lamao was just north of a river and a stone's throw west of the main east road, Route 110. It was an easy walk out to the shore of Manila Bay. A few men swam in the shallows on their time off, though not in the daytime, because of strafing planes. Perhaps sun and salt prevented fungus infections. We bathed in the river. We had soap, and we usually shaved twice a week. Colonel Miller was firm about that. We cut one another's hair, and before the surrender we were not lousy. Like Filipino villagers, we washed our own clothes on the rocks beside the river, where the sun dried and bleached them quickly.

All the water we drank was purified in Lister bags with Iodex pills. The straddle-trench latrines were kept meticulous. Men on latrine duty used lime and earth daily, and new latrines were dug often. Because of such care and the almost total absence of garbage, we were not troubled greatly by flies.

In the kitchen Bill Monroe and others worked and improvised constantly to give us two meals a day. Food issued by the quartermaster went first to the battalion headquarters and then was divided up for the separate companies. Colonel Miller made certain that every pinch was accounted for. Canned meat and canned potatoes, army staples, became an unobtainable luxury, and what little there was went into stews. Meat was replaced by canned salmon and occasionally canned sardine. Wheat flour, also in short supply, was used for gravy and ladled over the rice that became the staple issue. Occasionally, we got rice flour or we pounded raw rice into flour so that the cooks could give us rice pancakes with raw sugar—a feast for us.

Bataan was sparsely populated, with just the few villages on the coast, and very little food was grown there. Some rice paddies were cultivated, and the villagers fished both with nets and fish traps, but the fruits common in the Philippines were scarce on Bataan. We had no mango, no papaya, no guava, no pineapple, and no coconut—not even citrus fruits. We had no ascorbic-acid lemonade, a standard army food. Consequently, scurvy and night blindness became common. Sometimes we were issued canned peaches and canned tomatoes, which were especially welcome to season a stew. We still had large square tins of lard, which the cooks guarded like gold. We did not think about the old post-exchange luxuries such as chocolate, chewing gum, candy, and beer. A square meal was our main wish all the time.

Sometime in late January we slaughtered a carabao, the farm water buffalo of the Philippines. Later the quartermaster corps seized all the remaining carabao and slaughtered them at intervals, and we received occasional small issues of liver-tasting carabao meat. The calesa ponies brought in by the Filipino civilian refugees, crowded together near Mariveles, went into the pot also. A few pack mules and the remaining horses of the 26th Cavalry were butchered and divided up. Without refrigeration in that climate, the meat had to be cooked very soon after it was butchered. Sometimes our cooks were hard put to season meat that smelled high indeed.

By March, when we were on quarter rations, we began to forage for native plants and wildlife in earnest. Luckily, we were helped by Miguel García, called Mike, who had previously helped us build hospital beds. He knew the countryside well, and during the retreat into Bataan he was assigned to help the battalion find its way south. Then Major Canby placed him on special duty with one of the half-track reconnaissance units. He taught us which plants were not poisonous. He showed the cooks how to prepare the large, prickly soft globes of breadfruit and where to look for tender bamboo shoots for a stew. Even in the dry season Mike was able to find some green shoots. Occasionally, we had some of the long wild bananas. Fried lightly, they were edible but rather tasteless, until Mike showed the cooks how to serve them with raw sugar. Mike taught us to catch fish from Manila Bay and introduced us to the few Filipino fishermen, who did their best to help feed us as well as their families. We used bamboo grenades to stun fish in the water—not very sporting but necessary.

Once some of the Philippine Scouts caught a large python and enjoyed every morsel. Mike helped us find the large iguana lizards. One of them had bitten Sergeant Gerry Foley in the leg, and we were a little afraid of them, until we had eaten roast iguana tail à la Mike. It was as sweet and nutritious as roast suckling pig. Mike also showed us how to prepare the small monkeys. At first, for me, it seemed too much like eating a child, but toward the end I ate any bit I could get my hands on.

After coming out of an attack of malaria, I asked Mike what the Filipinos from the small country barrios did when they had malaria and had no quinine. When a malarial chill is upon you, you need to perspire. Then your fever usually lowers and the pain subsides for a while. Mike said, "Younger people run up and down the hills till they sweat. Older people drink tuba." Tuba is a potent wine made from rice and brown sugar. He grinned at me and said, "In your case, Fitz, it is regrettable that we have not tuba."

11

LAST DAYS

ON GOOD FRIDAY, April 3, 1942, the sky was cloudless, and the sun rose over Bataan with the promise of another scorching day for the American and Filipino troops. As soon as the sun was up, the heavily reinforced Japanese air force, bombers and fighters along with navy Zeros, came over in wave after wave. There was no letup.

During the last week of March a communiqué had been sent to all units from the recently appointed commander on Bataan, Major General Edward P. King, Jr., who had replaced General Wainwright, now in overall command on Corregidor. General King's message warned us that we could expect an all-out attack by the Japanese against the Pilar-Bagac front line at any time, along with attempted beach landings on the Manila Bay side of Bataan. The message described the constant arrival of Japanese replacements and new units of land, sea, and air forces from throughout the Japanese empire, including an observation balloon that was spotting for their artillery just behind the front lines. Landing barges had been assembled at the mouth of the Pampanga River, near the base of the Bataan Peninsula. Some of these, mounting 75-millimeter guns, were already trying to shell the beach defenses from the bay. General King ended his message by asking us to do our best. General King's expert, brilliant handling of the 155-millimeter artillery, vintage 1918, had done more to keep the Japanese army at bay than any other factor. He was without question the most capable and respected general in the Philippines.

About the middle of the morning, with planes still coming in overhead, the Japanese artillery opened up an awesome barrage, particularly against the strong point of the Pilar-Bagac line, the forward slopes of Mount Samat. For five hours the shelling was coordinated with continuous bombing and strafing. The Japanese planes had the sky to themselves, and our antiaircraft guns were few and obsolete.

Whenever American artillery tried to answer the shelling, it was pounced upon and destroyed by one or more Japanese planes.

Worst of all, the tropical brush and bamboo thickets quickly caught on fire. Apparently, some incendiary shells had been fired, but the vegetation was so dry that even ordinary shells could touch it off. The whole defensive position on the north side of Mount Samat became an inferno. Men, too weak from hunger and disease to run, burned to death. Whole regiments were finished, with many killed or burned and others groping their way toward the rear without their rifles. There was no strength, no fight left in them.

Before the Japanese tanks and infantry attacked, the last real battle for Bataan was over, although surrender was avoided for six more days. With obsolete equipment, half and quarter rations, and few medical supplies, the Battling Bastards of Bataan had held out for four months. They had become the Battered Bastards.

On that afternoon of April 3, the 31st Infantry Regiment moved out of its bivouac area near us at Lamao. One-third of the men had to be sent to the field hospitals. Many of the others left their makeshift regimental bivouac hospital to join their companies, only to fall out on the way, too weak to walk.

That night Japanese barges, mounting 75-millimeter artillery pieces, shelled our beach defense. We counterfired, and the barges withdrew. Good Friday had become Black Friday.

The next day the Japanese recommenced their artillery and air bombardment. They were unaware that they had already won. On the same day MacArthur, from his sanctuary in Australia 4,000 miles to the south, sent a lengthy plan to General Wainwright on Corregidor. Wainwright was to "prepare and execute an attack upon the enemy along the following general lines": he was to retake Olongapo on Subic Bay at the northern end of Bataan, and the "supplies seized at this base might well rectify the situation." Wainwright reported to both Washington and MacArthur that the situation was not hopeful: "I am forced to report that the troops on Bataan are fast folding up." MacArthur sent no change in orders. Wainwright gave the attack order to General King. King told the I Corps commander, General Jones, about the order to attack. Jones described the condition of his troops, in retreat and physically exhausted. King took upon himself the responsibility of not passing on to General Jones this order that could not possibly be obeyed.

The rollback of the front line continued, especially in the middle of II Corps, and the air and artillery attacks continued throughout April 4 and 5. We were told that MacArthur had dispatched fighter planes from the south (there were then three P-40s at the Del Monte airfield on Mindanao, about 400 miles from Bataan), and the bomb-pocked strip at Mariveles was alerted to receive them. As usual, nothing came.

A last-ditch counterattack was planned for April 6, and the troops who could still walk and hold a rifle made the attempt. Some of the units in the counterattack succeeded briefly in stemming and even driving back the Japanese flood a little way. The 45th Philippine Scouts, supported by Company C of the 194th Tank Battalion, were led by Colonel Miller in person, and they briefly drove a wedge into the advancing Japanese columns. But starvation and disease had already settled the issue. The Japanese continued to roll up II Corps, while fighting only a holding action against I Corps on the China Sea coast of Bataan. The counterattack faded.

By the afternoon of April 8 the dazed men of most units were plodding south toward Mariveles in the stifling heat on roads cratered by shells and bombs. Thick dust billowed in the air at every step, and the Japanese fighter planes were everywhere, strafing anything that moved. Men too weak to stumble off the roads or the trails were killed. The rest moved wearily on again, mostly without weapons or food or water or hope. At Lamao we stood exhausted by our tanks and half-tracks under the banyan trees and received orders that were immediately countermanded. Hungry and edgy, we watched in silence the tide of gaunt and worn men.

At about 4 P.M. a truck loaded with ammunition swung off the road and stopped under the trees in the middle of our area. We could hear the Japanese strafer coming down after him. Men fell off the road in front of us. The driver of the truck slammed open his door and jumped into one of our slit trenches. The strafing planes zoomed past with guns blazing, and the shells in the truck began to explode. It was like being attacked from all directions, as shells were blown off the truck to explode all around us. I jumped into a partially filled garbage pit. There wasn't time to be choosy, and I didn't notice it till afterward anyhow. Abruptly, the fireworks ended. The driver crawled out of the trench near the demolished, smoking ammunition truck and shook the dust off himself. He grinned out of his sunburnt, dirty face and said, "When they ask me where I was at the time of the surrender, I can always say I was where the shells were the thickest." And with that he nonchalantly walked back to the main road, hiked himself up over the side of a slow truck going south to Mariveles and thumbed his nose at us. We didn't know whether to laugh or curse.

Then we received Major Canby's orders to move south to a point near the Mariveles airstrip. We too joined the mass of men and vehicles. The road was lined with abandoned trucks, smashed trucks, pieces of equipment, and swollen bodies. All the way we could hear explosions. At Cabcaben we halted, while the large ammunition dumps were being blown up. Our whole world seemed to be blown apart. After another hour of slow travel we reached an assembly point where some of our battalion had already gathered in the darkness.

It was near midnight. I was dead tired, and I crawled out of a half-track and leaned against the nearest banyan tree. Suddenly I began to shake. I was sure I was beginning a malarial attack. I hung onto the tree. It too was shaking. The Bataan Peninsula was being rocked by an earthquake. The tremors died away. I wrapped my blanket around me and lay down to sleep, oblivious to the explosions of bombs, ammunition, and blown-up equipment.

12

SURRENDER

B Y THE NEXT MORNING, April 9, 1942, all the other members of the battalion had joined us. Colonel Miller and Company C had made it back from their final support of the 45th Philippine Scouts. He led us aside from our tanks and half-tracks and trucks to a clear space in the shade of some acacia trees. The men quietly gathered, most sitting on the grass, some leaning against trees. Colonel Miller faced us and told us formally what we already knew: we were surrendering. In his calm, blunt way, he explained how much we owed to General King, who, despite MacArthur's order to attack, had surrendered that morning in order to stop the slaughter of troops who no longer had the strength to resist. He ordered us to destroy our remaining equipment.

We turned our 37-millimeter guns against our tank and truck engines. We doused the smashed remains with gasoline and set them on fire. Small arms were smashed with rocks. We hammered our rifle and machine-gun bolts on rocks and threw them into the jungle. It was all done automatically, like a slow-motion bad dream.

At that moment, out of nowhere appeared a clean, freshly shaved, and neatly uniformed representative of the Army Finance Corps. He lined us up, as if nothing else in the world mattered, and doled out to each man a token payment of about 30 pesos ($15) for the past four months of combat. One of the corpsmen, Steve Joyce, announced grandly, "I think I'll go down to the corner drugstore and have a malted milk. I haven't had one for several days." Some of the men gambled their pesos away. I can't recall what I did with my payment—it meant so little to us on that day of surrender.

Colonel Miller sent Captain Clinton Quinlen, our quartermaster officer, to the nearest quartermaster supply depot to draw food for us for that day. Quinlen took along a few men who were skilled at "drawing" supplies. Sure enough, the officer in charge of the supply depot wanted the battalion roster for the day before he would release a single crumb of food. The Japanese were expected at any hour, and yet the red-tape regulations had to be obeyed. Captain Quinlen argued at first coolly and then with angry dramatics, keeping the supply officer's attention while Quinlen's aides went to work. Finally, the officer gave Quinlen a modest amount of canned goods. Quinlen's aides had taken a great deal more. By the next day all the supply depots would be in Japanese hands.

That afternoon we bathed in a nearby stream. Clothes were issued from each company's supply truck. I was fortunate to receive a new pair of well-fitting shoes. The medics gave out what was left of the medicine to those who needed it most. Dr. Leo Schneider gave twelve quinine pills to anyone who, like me, had had two or more malaria attacks in Bataan.

In the early evening the cooks served the best meal we had eaten in months. Then the rest of the canned goods acquired by Quinlen and his men were distributed equally to each member of the battalion, regardless of rank. As we sat around the embers of that last cook fire, I was asked to lead the group in a few songs, and we sang "Old Kentucky Home" and "Long, Long Trail Awinding."

Major Canby got up and said, "Tomorrow may come early." We needed no urging. We wrapped up in our blankets and went to sleep with a full stomach for the first time in many long weeks.

13

THE HIKE BEGINS

THE MORNING HEAT of another clear tropical day, April 10, had settled down on the dusty, shell-packed airstrip in Mariveles. General King's exhausted, diseased, and starving American and Filipino soldiers waited for the Japanese in the strange silence that followed the fighting on Bataan.

The first Japanese column came marching out of the jungle on a trail only a few yards from where I stood with tankers and other soldiers. The Japanese troops looked almost as exhausted as we were. Near the front of the column a Japanese private stumbled and fell. The officer halted the column, dismounted from his horse, and ordered the soldier to get up. When the soldier remained on the ground, the officer seized his sword in his scabbard and repeatedly hit the soldier on the head with the ornamented hilt of his sword. Eventually, the soldier strained to his feet, with the blood running in furrows down through the sweat and dust on his face. He swayed and reached around the shoulders of two comrades, and the column moved forward to the opposite side of the airstrip.

As if nothing had happened, the officer strolled to a log nearby and sat down to clean the blood from the hilt of his sword. Seeing two Americans near him, he spoke casually to them in excellent English. I was one of them. Later I realized that he was acting normally. If we had been able to comprehend the traditional values behind his actions, we would have understood: the soldier, a servant of the emperor, was never tired, was never exhausted, and never fell—most certainly not in the presence of the enemy, a captive, dishonored enemy. It was unthinkable and had to be punished immediately as a lesson to the others—a lesson not just to the peers of the Japanese private, not just to the officer's superiors who would punish him if he did not punish the private swiftly and severely, but a lesson to the captured enemy that we will treat him as we treat our own. We can, in honor, do no less.

A small group of Japanese soldiers, their rifles with bayonets fixed and carried at port across their chests, came toward us. In good English an interpreter told us to line up in columns of four, facing east with our hands up. Some of the soldier guards counted us off in groups of 100. The interpreter left, and the guards motioned to us to march toward Cabcaben and to keep our hands up. Then we realized we were being photographed. The guards beamed, and cameras clicked—proof for Manila and Tokyo that the men of General King were captured. One of these photographs appeared on the jacket of Colonel Miller's book *Bataan Uncensored*, subsequently in Stanley L. Falk's *Bataan: The March of Death*, on the cover of the paperback edition of Eric Morris's *Corregidor: The End of the Line*, and in David E. Scherman's *Life Goes to War: A Picture History of World War II*, which misidentifies the photo's location as Corregidor.

We had marched about a half a mile when the guards ordered us to stop. We heard cries of pain from a group behind us. The guards motioned us to turn right face and hold out our hands for inspection. This was the first of many shakedowns for rings and watches. I held out my hands, and my tank wristwatch was very noticeable. One man a few files down from me was wearing a wedding band. The guard took his wristwatch. Then he smiled and gestured at the ring. "Wifu?" he said. The American soldier nodded, and the guards moved on. Immediately I turned my college graduation ring so that the band was uppermost, to look like a wedding ring.

Then the same guard stood in front of me. Behind him stood another guard silently scrutinizing my watch and ring. The first guard took my watch from my outstretched left arm. Then he pointed to my ring, and he smiled and said, "Wifu." By now it was a statement rather than a question.

But the other guard stepped forward and gestured that I should turn my hands over. As I hesitated, he abruptly barked two words that would set our nerves on edge for the next three and a half years: "Kura! Baka!" The first guard, his expression hardening, snapped the bayonet off the muzzle of his rifle.

Standing just behind me, Sergeant Scotty McDonald, a tank commander, said, "For God's sake, Fitz, give him the ring. They just cut the finger off someone because he tried to keep his ring."

Captured American soldiers at Mariveles Airfield, April 10, 1942, soon to begin the Bataan Death March.

I never took off a ring so fast in my life. I held it out to the guard. He slowly put his bayonet over the muzzle of his rifle, snapped it into place, and took my ring. The two of them never took their eyes off me. They talked together briefly, and I was sure they were discussing a punishment for me. Just then, a Japanese officer came by and barked out orders to all the guards, who stopped searching us and motioned us to face left and march toward Cabcaben. "Speedo! Speedo!"

In the frequently reproduced photo mentioned above, these two guards, wearing caps, smile out from the left-hand side of the picture. The one wearing glasses is the guard who told me to turn over my hands. Slightly behind him to his right, with his rifle on his shoulder, is the guard who was content to overlook the wedding band of any man who had a "wifu." In the photograph I am standing among the American soldiers, my hands unraised, my doughboy helmet at a somewhat rakish angle, and my face partially obscured by a soldier's raised left hand.

We marched toward Cabcaben for a couple of miles. We were then

Bernard FitzPatrick (circled) at the beginning of the Bataan Death March, April 10, 1942.

turned around and marched back toward Mariveles for about the same distance. We were halted and told to fall out alongside the road. Although it was noon and the sun beat down mercilessly, we had some shade from a few trees and high bushes. I sat in the shade and took a sparing drink from my canteen and ate part of a can of C ration that I had in my old musette bag.

Soon we were ordered to fall in again and were marched this time all the way to Cabcaben airfield, six miles or more. It became cooler near dusk. More and more prisoners were arriving. We were herded together on the airfield, with enough space to lie down. The guards patrolled the edges of the field. I took another sparing drink from the canteen and finished the can of C ration.

As the darkness increased, guards with flashlights walked among us. Occasionally, with a thrust of a bayonet they forced men to move closer together. A flashlight's beam picked out the face of Eddie King of the 194th Battalion headquarters. Dazed and indrawn with fatigue, I hadn't noticed him. He had been severely wounded in the leg early in the Bataan campaign and had lately been released from Hospital Number One. We talked quietly. Then, because our blankets had been taken from us and that night was unusually cold, we curled up close to a few other friends to keep warm.

The guards roused us early the next morning, April 11, counted us off into groups of 100, and marched us north toward Lamao. The road,

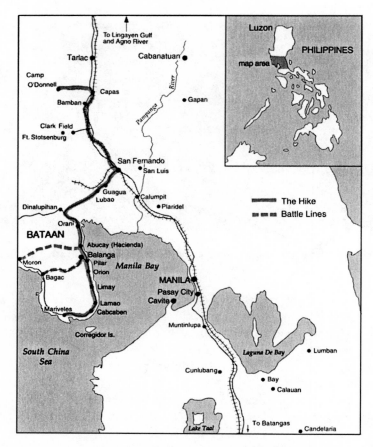

The Death March and Some Combat Areas of the Philippines. Map by Brian Kowalski and Steve Leach, Cartography Lab of the Geography Department of the University of Minnesota.

recently bombed and shelled, became rougher. More men came from every trail and side road. Roughly 10,000 Americans and more than 60,000 Filipinos had begun the Hike, as we called it, and in this first half of the march, the Filipinos and Americans were intermingled. I saw a Filipino lying dead by the road in faded blue hospital pajamas. His leg had been amputated. I saw more hospital cases. They were from Hospital Number Two, west of Cabcaben. The day before, the Japanese had told them they were free. Despite the pleading of Colonel Jack Schwartz, a senior doctor whom I greatly respected, many patients left the hospital and started north. Many of them died the first day.

Five fellow members of the 194th Tank Battalion (forefront) during the Bataan Death March, April 10, 1942. None of these men survived.

On the road from Cabcaben to Lamao we heard the first salvos of the Japanese artillery against Corregidor. More and more heavy equipment was coming down from the north. We were halted beside the road while heavy guns were hauled past. Some of the prisoners who had been in the artillery were sure they could hear counterfire from either Corregidor or one of the other island forts in Manila Bay. Unfortunately, this was true. The shelling was from Corregidor, and although they did their best to avoid hitting Hospital Number Two and were effective against the Japanese artillery concentration, they were also effective against the Filipino and American prisoners plodding through. Among those killed from our battalion was a close friend and an able young officer named Lieutenant Ray Bradford.

The marines and army and navy defenders on the island fortress of Corregidor would now face the full fury of the Japanese war machine. Except for an occasional bombing, the past four months had been relatively safe for them, as long as we had held Bataan. They were to be spared the Death March, which would be long over by the time Corregidor surrendered on May 6, 1942.

"Death Marchers Drink from Mud Holes," a drawing by Ben Steele.

We reached Lamao about noon. Hot and exhausted, we were glad to be halted beside the road to allow more heavy equipment to go past. We were not given any food, but by chance we were stopped by an artesian well familiar to us. The guards did not notice us drinking and filling our canteens. Other units were not so lucky: their guards made them stay in position.

Late in the afternoon as we approached Limay, we could see the devastation of the bombing and artillery in the final days of fighting. All the tropical vegetation near the highway was obliterated. A haze hung over the land to the left of us. In the distance fires were still burning from the incendiary bombs dropped during the initial Good Friday attack. In the ditches and torn-up land, large crows were gorging themselves on the bodies of the dead. Crows were circling above our column. I was walking beside Tennessee Solsbee from Company A of the 194th Tank Battalion. Tennessee looked up at the dark, circling birds and muttered, "You all go away, big birds. I'm not fixing to die yet."

The Filipino and American prisoners coming down from the

mountain trails onto the main road along Manila Bay swelled the groups so that order became impossible. Prisoners slumped to the ground. Some rested and staggered on, and some died where they fell. Some prisoners drank from the carabao wallows, green and scummed over and sometimes fouled by the bloated body of a dead soldier. Because of their terrible thirst combined with malaria or dengue fever, some prisoners ignored the danger of dysentery from drinking such water.

Late in the afternoon several hundred of us were marched to a nearby field. We were crowded together, and guards were posted for the night. The rest of the column was marched north. We were given no food at Limay, but I was thankful to lie down and sleep.

14

VITAMIN STICKS

THE NEXT MORNING, April 12, we were roused before sunrise and told to fall in, in a column of fours. I took one of my twelve quinine pills with a sip of water from my canteen. The guards said that we would be fed when we got to Balanga and that many of us would then be put into trucks for the trip to San Fernando or all the way to the prison camp near Capas.

We were marching by the time the sun came up, and the pace was much faster that day. The scorching heat and the lack of food and water sapped the prisoners' strength. When men fell, they were ordered to rise, and if they didn't, they were usually bayoneted and left where they were.

My group reached Orion about noon. I remembered from our combat days that there was an artesian well near the road. I had already learned that a canteen neck was too narrow to catch water from the spigot of such wells. So I loosened my canteen cup from the bottom of my canteen. As we came near the well, we ran and jostled for the water. The guards yelled incomprehensible commands and swung their rifle butts, but many of us reached the spigot. I was able to fill about two thirds of my canteen cup. As we fell back into ranks, I poured the water into my almost empty canteen.

The guards counted us off into groups like our original hundreds. I was in the last group to march out. We had only one guard now, and he seemed almost as tired as we were. He let the pace slacken. Around 4 P.M., shortly after we had passed through Pilar and were a mile or two south of Balanga, our guard said, "Yasumi." ("Rest.") He motioned us toward a lone tree by the roadside. Almost blind and cooked from the sun and dust, we could hardly believe our luck at the chance to rest in some shade.

The guard, a private, had some pickles in a jar. He did not know

"The Stragglers," a drawing by Ben Steele.

any English, but he offered me one of these small pickles. It was slightly bitter and shocking to my tongue but unbelievably welcome. Then he gave me a sip of water from his canteen. He took off one of his army shoes and showed me a huge blister on his right heel. "Dame, dame." ("Bad, no good.") He sat there easing his feet, another lonely soldier worn out with fighting in Bataan and bone tired from plodding north on that dusty, hot, rough road. He pulled some papers out of his pocket and carefully showed me worn photos of his wife and their two small children.

Then, with a snarl of overloaded brakes and an enveloping cloud of dust, a captured American truck slammed to a halt in front of us. A dozen Japanese soldiers in nearly immaculate uniforms jumped down from the truck, screaming and yelling, "Kura! Kura! Speedo! Speedo!" and waving looted golf clubs and their regular "vitamin-stick" clubs. These rear-echelon marvels harangued our poor guard, who hastily stuffed his feet into his shoes. They beat him with their golf clubs and vitamin sticks until he roused us and we all started grimly north again. After a few more imprecations incomprehensible to us, the soldiers piled back into their truck. Gears clashed, and off they jolted, south toward Mariveles.

As we entered what was left of Balanga, empty skeletal buildings hammered by constant artillery, my morale dropped. All was confusion. Prisoners from I Corps, on the China Sea side of Bataan, had come east across the all-season road from Bagac to Balanga. Most of them had come ten or more miles as we had. Prisoners were milling about the dusty streets by the thousands. No Japanese seemed to know what to do. The guards barked unintelligible commands and beat prisoners without mercy. The Japanese had expected only half as many prisoners and had no plans for dealing with the thousands of civilian refugees arriving from the southern tip of Bataan. At Balanga, the capital of Bataan province, the Japanese were apparently supposed to sort us out.

My group passed in a single file through a group of arrogant "superior privates," with three stars on their collars, and a gang of buck-private guards. It was another shakedown. These soldiers were well dressed and sure of themselves. They were not the tired unshaven combat men who had taken us in charge two days before. These men were quick with their vitamin sticks, and our new guards soon were just as quick with the rifle butt, the bayonet, or the bullet.

As I passed through the shakedown line, I was relieved of my razor, razor blades, and the knife and fork from my mess kit. I was allowed to keep the spoon, the mess kit, the canteen cup and canteen, the carrying belt, and my steel helmet. The small musette bag hanging unobtrusively over my shoulder wasn't even searched. Others were deprived of all of their personal belongings.

The town had become so overcrowded that in the fenced enclosures, built for the anticipated smaller number of prisoners, we had hardly room to sit. My group, along with some others, was herded to an open field, dry rice paddies, just north of town. Here the guards packed us away for the night. As each man lay down, he was prodded by a bayonet until he was face down and tight against the next man. The rice paddies became large sardine tins. At the edge of the paddies was shade from a grove of mango trees, all bearing fruit. I flopped down between prisoners I did not know. It was late in the afternoon, and we were so exhausted we didn't even speak.

Suddenly, a Japanese yelled something. I looked up. A young

Filipino soldier was stumbling through the prisoners toward the mango trees. The guard yelled again. The hungry and thirsty and probably fevered Filipino soldier kept walking. The guard raised his rifle and fired three times. The boy fell, squirmed a little, and lay still. I lay back down.

In the warm, tropic night in the dry season, it was not a great hardship to sleep in the open, even on the hard ground. Bone weary and long starved, men fell into sleep as into a coma.

In the clear gray of the early morning, already flushed with heat and dust from the road, the English-speaking guards ordered us to fall in. "Move out. Rice, very good." One guard called out, "Messie-messie," and rubbed his stomach. On each side of me lay a body dead and cold. The paddies were spotted with still bodies counterfeiting sleep. The crows circled overhead patiently.

The guards formed us into lines for our first Japanese meal since the surrender. The cooked dry rice was ladled from the pots called kawalis and from wheelbarrows. I had my mess kit ready. The man behind me tapped me on the shoulder. He said, "Would you trade me your tin hat for my pith helmet? During the shakedown yesterday the bastards took everything I owned." The trade seemed a good one for both of us. I got a lighter hat, and he got not only a helmet but something to hold water and food. That issue of cooked rice was small, but we savored every grain. The pinch of salt on the rice was even more welcome. We had not known how much we craved it.

After we went through the rice line, we were immediately placed in a column of fours in groups of 100. The same group of superior privates, the shakedown artists of the previous afternoon, made a careful inspection and separated the Filipinos from the Americans. From now on we were closely supervised. Each group had a prisoner appointed as leader and had at least one Japanese guard and usually several. There were no latrines, and the whole town smelled like a sewer. Huge flies were collecting.

The sun blazed full force. We became more and more dehydrated. Our lips cracked from the heat and the dust. Some were crazed for water. I was very lucky to have a canteen, a little water, and some quinine to hold the malaria at bay. I too craved the unclean water in carabao wallows and stagnant pools. Some who drank that water were so weak that they lay half in the water and expired. Prisoners who drank from these wallows very quickly showed signs of nausea and dysentery. Prisoners fell and were helped to their feet by other prisoners. Some fell again, and there would come the commands from the guard, and if the prisoner could not continue, there would come the bayonet, a flash in the bright sun, through the prisoner's neck. Those of us who kept walking were so starved, thirsty, and dehydrated that we were emotionally and mentally numb. Beyond Balanga the Hike became hazy for me and many others. One remembers moments, pictures, and the endless mechanical action of forcing oneself to put one foot after another down the road.

Along the road north to Orani, however, at some small barrio near Abucay, I well remember the Filipino women, old people, and children standing by the road. Some boys tossed us rice cakes and sugared bananas wrapped in nipa-palm leaves. The guards set upon the boys. Women placed on the road small earthenware jars full of cool water. The guards kicked the jars over or smashed them with their rifle butts. The women cried, and the old men rubbed their eyes as they wept. In many other barrios, regardless of whether the prisoners were Filipino or American, people stood beside the road with jars and tin cans set out for us. And they tossed us bananas, rice cakes, rice cookies, eggs, and even hard candy. Many prisoners took heart and lived because of those bits of food and hasty gulps of water from the jars that weren't knocked over. The barrio people gave unstintingly from their poverty. Clubs and rifle butts were often their reward.

As we left a large barrio north of Orani, where the shops gave way to open land, an elderly Chinese merchant in a dark, wide-sleeved robe was standing rooted by the side of the road. His arms were crossed and his hands out of sight in his sleeves. The Japanese guards ignored him. Occasionally one of his hands would dart out of a sleeve and put a rice cookie or some other bit of food into a prisoner's hand. He smiled faintly and nodded ever so slightly, as his hand vanished into the sleeve again.

Our column of walking dead shuffled into Orani a couple of hours before sunset. The heat was still violent. A stench of death and feces pierced our nostrils, as insensitive as they had become. Our group was at the head of this day's seemingly endless column. We were herded into a fenced area with some shade from a row of dusty acacia trees. Near the fence at one end were unburied dead from the groups before us. There were a few straddle-trench latrines, crawling with maggots. We crowded around a water spigot near the enclosure entrance. I filled my canteen cup and, with shaking care, poured the water into my canteen.

As the first group into the enclosure, we were herded to the far end in the shade of the trees. Eventually, for most, there wasn't enough space to lie down. Prisoners with dysentery were urged to use the straddle trenches, but although they tried to reach them, many had no control and defecated where they stood. I slept in a stupor that night, half-sitting, half-lying.

15

VAYA CON DIOS

AS WE LEFT the next morning, April 14, the guards issued a small ration of rice and a pinch of salt. I ate the salt first because I had an almost uncontrollable craving for salt. Back in the enclosure, clumps of bodies still lay sprawled on the filthy ground.

After Orani the land became flatter and more open. There were few shade trees, and the heat became more intense. Time and again we were forced to the side of the road to make way for convoys of trucks loaded with Japanese soldiers to help besiege Corregidor. Heavy guns, both tractor drawn and on mobile mounts, moved past. The chalky dust swirled around us. Some prisoners, too weak to get out of the road fast enough, were knocked down or run over. On two occasions I saw Japanese soldiers lean out of the trucks and hit prisoners with rifle butts or long bamboo poles. These men were reinforcement troops who had never faced us in combat.

Some men simply plodded off the highway and were hidden by dust and overlooked by the guards. Phil Tripp of the 194th became detached from his group, lay down off the road for a whole day, and then started walking again. Brownell Cole of the 31st Infantry knew every inch of the road up the Bataan Peninsula, having driven it many times in his truck. After a guard had walked past him, Brownie dove off the road into a pool of water in a huge ditch. He scrambled away from the road and behind a bamboo thicket. Here, next to a stream, he opened a can of C ration, set the can down, reached behind for his canteen, and discovered a bloated corpse, unrecognizable as friend or foe. He filled his canteen, ate his C ration, and slept. A day later he rejoined the march.

From Orani to Lubao was the longest day's march of all, 15 miles, not a very long hike for a man in good shape. Somewhere on that endless road, at a barrio near Dinalupihan, Bill McKeon, Phil Brain, and I were plodding along abreast of one another. Like a graceful broken-field runner, a small Filipino boy darted behind one of the guards and passed like a flash in front of us, thrusting a small watermelon into Phil Brain's hands. The boy eeled past to the other side of the column and slipped away. A guard cursed and chased him but soon gave up. Phil held the melon close to his chest, and when the guards relaxed again, he broke the melon into pieces. We ate it rind and all. Bill McKeon muttered irrepressibly, "Haven't you got a little salt for it?"

As we neared Lubao, friendly Filipinos lined the road. They set out tin water containers big enough to dip a canteen cup. They tossed us mangoes and sugar-covered bananas wrapped in leaves. Some of the guards allowed us to keep the food and drink the water.

Just inside the town of Lubao, we were herded into the single entrance of a fenced enclosure about the size of a football field. In the middle of this area was a sheet-iron warehouse. I was almost oblivious to the smell of feces ground into the earth. Men were already packed into the outside yard, and we were forced inside the warehouse. I noticed a water spigot near the wall at one side, but I was so exhausted that I slumped down on the cement, half sitting against the metal wall. I did not want to lie down. I was afraid of not being able to get up, of being taken for dead. It was getting dark when another prisoner awakened me. He had lost all his equipment in one of the shakedowns. "Give me your canteen," he said, "and I'll try to get some water."

I fumbled at my belt and found my canteen cup. "Here's my canteen cup," I said. "Drink what you need and bring some back for me." After a while he came back and held out my filled cup. I sipped water slowly and thankfully and swallowed my quinine tablet for that day. Then I poured the rest of the cup into my canteen, put the canteen and cup in my musette bag, fastened it around my neck, and fell heavily asleep.

The guards' shouted commands roused us early the next morning, April 15. We were told that we would walk eight miles to San Fernando, where the railroad trains or the trucks would take us the rest of the way to a prison camp. We joined a long, slow line as rice and salt were rationed to us. The line then wound out of the enclosure to groups forming on the road.

In an open space near us, two prisoners had dug a shallow grave for a friend. They had persuaded a guard to give them a shovel, an unusual act for which the guard might have been reprimanded. As they started to cover their friend in the grave, the body moved. The guard impatiently gestured for them to hurry. They protested. The guard gestured violently toward the shovel and then at the prisoner's head. The other prisoner held up his hands in protest. The guard poised his bayonet at the stomach of the prisoner with the shovel. He raised the shovel. I turned my head and walked on. When I looked back, the shallow grave was covered with dirt.

Later in Cabanatuan Prison Camp, Lieutenant Henry G. Lee portrayed our feelings on the Death March in his poem "Death of a Friend":

> So you are dead. The easy words contain
> No sense of loss, no sorrow, no despair.
> Thus, hunger, thirst, fatigue combine to drain
> All feeling from our hearts. The endlesss glare,
> The brutal heat anesthetize the mind.
> I cannot mourn you now. I lift my load.
> The suffering column moves. I leave behind
> Only another corpse beside the road.

As we marched slowly out of Lubao, the road became rutted. The asphalt had been chewed up by the loaded trucks and heavy artillery and other equipment moving south. Many of the prisoners' shoes had worn completely through, and the hot asphalt burned their feet. One prisoner asked me to help him tear his shirt in two. Awkwardly, because we were both weak, we tore the shirt, and he tied the halves around his blistered feet. For once, the guards did not interfere.

This day's march became a blur to me because there was no shade in the flat, open countryside. The sun was blazing hot. Men fell and lay still. Fewer Filipinos stood by the road. A Japanese order had forbade their helping us. But when our column passed between the small nipa houses of a barrio, some people risked the anger of the guards, who were bored and mechanical now. Some guards ceased to notice the Filipinos' gifts of water and food, but other guards beat them into insensibility. Some Filipinos died for their charity to us.

From the blurred memory of that day, I recall a Filipino boy slipping me a piece of sugar cane and then running back behind a house. In another barrio an old man, erect and calm beside the road, put a small cake of raw sugar in my hand. The expression on his face never changed when he said, "Vaya con Dios, compadre." His serene dignity made the guards ignore him.

About the middle of the afternoon, with the heat shimmering above the road, we reached the capital of Pampanga province, San Fernando, where we had gone on weekend passes before the war. The Japanese had several fenced enclosures: a large schoolyard, an old factory, a cock-fight arena, and a pottery shed. I was shoved through an opening in the fence around the pottery shed. The yard was nearly empty, but another group had been moved out earlier that day, leaving the smell of dysentery.

The sun was like a block of cement on my head. I stumbled into the pottery shed and sat against the wall and slept. Later a man shook me. He had a canteen but no mess kit. He told me the Japanese were issuing rice, and water was available. I trusted him with my mess kit, and when he returned, we split the sizable portion of salted rice and drank from his canteen. I was too done in to ask him his name.

We stayed in the pottery shed that night, all the next day, and a second night. Rice and salt were issued to us in fairly generous portions at dusk and early in the morning. The soldier who had shared my mess kit, I now learned, was Jeremiah Collins, a sergeant in the 31st Infantry. We stuck together when we were moved out on the morning of April 17, to be taken by train almost all the way to our final destination, Camp O'Donnell.

After the extra day's rest, I was glad to be up and out of the maggoty, fetid pottery shed. We marched straight to the railroad that would take us to Capas, the town near Camp O'Donnell. Some of the prisoners were lighthearted at the thought of riding in a railroad coach after the days of agonized walking. Our spirits dropped when the guards began stuffing us into the boxcars.

The boxcar became so tightly jammed that one stood tight against other prisoners. The doors were slammed shut. Jerry Collins and I, facing the wooden sides of the car, immediately used a mess-kit handle to dig a hole between two boards, so we were able to breathe a little. There was no hysteria. One prisoner said that we should not talk, so as to conserve oxygen. Men with dysentery defecated where they stood. Some men died and were held on their feet by the pressure against the other prisoners.

After about an hour the train jerked in preparation for moving off.

The two guards assigned to our car slid open the door and sat with their backs to us. The cooler fresh air was a lifesaver to those who had lapsed into unconsciousness. The men who needed fresh air the most were slowly moved toward the open door, and the motion of the train created a welcome airflow.

It was about a three-hour train trip from San Fernando to Capas, a distance of about 25 miles. At each barrio the train slowed down and often had to go through switches. Filipinos crowded up close and threw us water bottles, bananas, tomatoes, brown-sugar cakes, and sugar cane. At first our guards threw everything back into the crowd. Then, prompted by the example of the Filipinos, they helped the sick. But in the steel boxcars, some with closed doors, lacking oxygen and sweltering in the heat of the sun and the crowded bodies, many men died.

At Capas we were to trudge nine miles to Camp O'Donnell, to complete our trek of 110 miles from Mariveles. Men fell out of the box-cars into the air. Filipino civilians had gathered in hundreds, trying to catch a glimpse of relatives. Completely fearless of the guards, they pressed food into our hands and ladled water for us. A group of older people came straight to our leaders and assured us that our dead would receive proper burial.

Part Two

THE SAMURAI
AND MACARTHUR

16

SURVIVAL OF THE SAMURAI

O N THE HIKE we were forced to march or accept a bayonet, and
in the prison camps we suffered further beatings and humilia-
tions. The Japanese treatment of war prisoners was brutal, according
to Western standards, but the motives can be traced to the conven-
tions of the Japanese army and to attitudes inflamed by the heat of
battle.

The Japanese soldier had been trained from childhood to feel a
lifelong obligation to his parents, his family, his village, his work, and
most of all his emperor. The army, as the protector of the throne and
as the representative of the emperor, demanded a new intensity of the
soldier's obligations.

The training of the conscripted Japanese soldier was harsh. Every
punishment was immediate and physical, and there was no appeal to
a court-martial. Each rank had complete authority over the rank
below. At Cabanatuan Prison Camp, we saw the Japanese training
newly conscripted soldiers. The slightest mistake earned severe punishment. We saw soldiers beaten unconscious, brought to with a bucket
of water, and beaten again. The Japanese noncommissioned officers
often beat their inferiors with the flat of their swords, usually scab-
barded. Both noncoms and the two-star and three-star privates used
the long, thin club that we prisoners called a vitamin stick. Sometimes
a whole group was beaten for one man's infraction of the rules.
Presumably, peer pressure would then cure him of his error.

Many Japanese themselves considered the army and navy training
to be both brutal and demanding. Only the desire for success and the
fear of being shamed by failure could have carried the Japanese soldier
or sailor through such training. And this training turned him into an
automaton who never questioned authority and who did only what he
was explicitly ordered to do. This training in complete obedience to all

77

orders produced a fighting man who expected to win and was usually willing to sacrifice himself. The soldier was also trained to make do with only the bare essentials of military equipment and to conserve water and live off the land.

Officers were also to follow the Five Words included in the Imperial Rescript of the Emperor Meiji in 1873: (1) A soldier must do his duty to his country; (2) A soldier must be courteous; (3) A soldier must show courage in war; (4) A soldier must keep his word; and (5) A soldier must live simply. These words were taken with enormous seriousness. The concept of simplicity was reflected by the austere Japanese uniform for all grades. The Five Words, however, did not prescribe how an officer should treat his men. He could order them to make attacks that were suicidal, or he could suggest that a subordinate pay for an error by committing ritual suicide.

Above all, the Japanese soldier was taught that he must have seishen, the self-sacrificing spirit that conquers even materially superior opposition. The Japanese high command believed that a soldier properly infused with seishen would be equal to ten enemy soldiers. The swift success of the Japanese forces during the Russo-Japanese War of 1905 and the many campaigns against the Chinese in the 1930s had encouraged an almost mystical belief in seishen. This confidence was shaken by a savage defeat at the hands of the Russians in the Nomonhan area of Manchuria in August 1939. The Japanese admitted to 18,000 casualties and put all reports under strict security. A discussion followed: Should the Japanese army modernize and increase its firepower or continue to count on seishen? Prime Minister Hideki Tojo assured the emperor that seishen would carry the day, and so it was decided. In another respect the battle at Nomonhan was even more decisive: henceforth, Japanese expansion would be aimed to the south toward Malaya and Indonesia and not to the north toward Russia.

The bushido code, the code of the samurai, had centuries of tradition behind it. In feudal Japan the emperor had been eclipsed and used as a figurehead for the shogun, a military dictator who lived in Yedo, later renamed Tokyo. Here he ruled absolutely through the allegiance of clan leaders, or daimyo, like the almost autonomous barons of England in the fourteenth century. Each clan had its private professional army of samurai, who became the highest class in the Japanese caste system. They had the power of life and death over the classes below them, although they owned little other than their swords. They maintained their status by absolute loyalty to their daimyo. If their lord was killed, they became ronin, or masterless men, unclassed until they could serve another lord.

From the early medieval times the samurai's attitude toward capture or surrender was strikingly different from the attitude of the Western European knight, who followed rules for the courteous treatment and ransom of a captive. In Japan the samurai sought death rather than capture. If captured alive, he could expect brutal treatment, since the Japanese victor killed not only the vanquished daimyo but also his relatives and samurai retainers, to avoid a vendetta, a feud led by the slain lord's retainers. The Japanese never devised a system, like the German Wergeld, of paying a family to prevent the clan from seeking vengeance. Furthermore, unlike the tales of medieval knights, the epic stories of the samurai are not romantic.

Under the Tokugawa shogunate the system of the daimyos and their samurai lasted for 250 years, a time of stability and prosperity. The system provided security for the Japanese until Commodore Perry arrived in 1853 and opened Japan to the Western world. Then the feudal lords met to plan the future, and they made many changes. The shogunate and allegiance to the clans were abolished. The emperor was moved from Kyoto to Tokyo, the new capital. The year 1868 inaugurated the Meiji restoration, after the name that the emperor took when he ascended the throne. Many of the young samurai and the forward-looking merchants threw themselves into the formation of a new Japan. The slogan of the new era was "national prosperity and military power."

Zealous men were sent to study the ways, institutions, and techniques of the great powers. They admired Germany under Bismarck, and in 1889 the emperor presented the people with a new constitution modeled on Germany's. At first Japan relied on French military advisers, but after the Franco-Prussian War, German advisers helped organize the new Japanese army. For developing a navy, Japan turned to British advisers. In 1873 the Japanese instituted conscription for military service. The proud samurai were ordered not to wear their swords in public, and soon they were dissolved as a military caste. The samuari rose in a futile series of revolts. Revolt to preserve the throne or correct some evil was based on the concept of gekokujo, power of the lower ranks over the upper, a paradox in the hierarchical, authoritarian system of Japan.

The power of the army and navy in the Japanese government was ensured by an imperial ordinance in 1900. Previously, the minister of war, the minister of the navy, and the army and navy chiefs of staff had already had direct access to the emperor. The imperial ordinance of 1900 increased this power by requiring that the military ministers must be generals or admirals on active duty. If the army or navy refused to appoint a minister, a cabinet could not be formed. Civilian control became extremely difficult.

In the late 1920s and early 1930s the army further influenced politics. In seizing Manchuria in 1931, the Kwantung army acted entirely without authority from the Japanese government, which was then forced by popular opinion to accept a fait accompli. Officers of the supreme command jokingly gave the nickname "Kwantung Army" to any group that ignored the dictates of the supreme command.

As the worldwide Depression settled on Japan, unrest in the army grew more serious. Many of the young officers came from poverty-stricken families in rural Japan. These young officers formed army cliques that sought to control the policies of the army and the government. Some generals served as leaders of these groups in dangerous power struggles. Many of the Japanese officers were impressed by the rise of Nazi Germany and the enormous power of the German military leaders.

17

DISHONOR

IF THE JAPANESE SOLDIER became a prisoner of war—a horyo or dishonored captive—he expected to be killed. He would, theoretically, rather kill himself. If he were disgraced by capture, his family and his village would feel the disgrace. His name would be struck from the village records. If he died disgraced, his ashes could not be brought back to the Yasukuni Jinja, the great military shrine that honors Japan's war heroes. The men from a district were assigned to the same military units, and so this social pressure was maintained even far from home.

A soldier raised from the mines or the farms wore a uniform that demanded the utmost respect. Despite the harsh training, the Japanese soldier had achieved a position requiring deference from all civilians. At the Yawata steel mill, where I was later interned, even the guards received a deep bow from every grade of civilian employee. When a soldier achieved success in combat, he was almost revered in his village. The Japanese soldier expected deference everywhere, in the Philippines, Burma, and China. If formal courtesies were not offered, he felt insulted—for himself, his unit, his army, and his emperor. Japan eventually suffered because of this cock-of-the-walk attitude, which at the beginning of the war had encouraged military morale. The ordinary people in the towns and villages came to hate the military. The well-clothed and well-fed soldiers were a sharp contrast to the patched and hungry civilians.

We war prisoners soon learned to bow and almost forgot the salute. Many war prisoners were still bowing after the war when they were back in the United States. In late 1945 I was invited to a dance at Schick General Hospital in Clinton, Iowa, and my date asked me not to act like a war prisoner. When she introduced me to her commanding officer, however, I automatically placed my hands in position

81

at the center line of my trousers and bowed. They passed it off as a joke—even though former war prisoners at the hospital were not supposed to attend these dances.

The Japanese scorn for materialism and the concept of a brave death as a spiritual victory made the Japanese relatively unconcerned about the soldier who was wounded or ill with malaria. There was a disgrace in being sick at all. When the Japanese army had to retreat, hospitalized soldiers were given hand grenades to finish themselves off or were shot by the medical personnel. Often Japanese prisoners concealed a hand grenade to destroy both themselves and a captor. Therefore, the Japanese regarded their treatment of the American and Filipino prisoners on the Hike as harsh but appropriate. To them we were horyo. We should have welcomed death in a last stand. That we wished to send our names to the United States and our families seemed to them shameful.

Our harsh treatment was also a result of the regimen of the Japanese troops. The most austere conditions in all training were considered beneficial. So Colonel Masanobu Tsuji transported Japanese troops to the Philippines by jamming men into a ship three to a mat, an area of six by three feet, for a week's voyage in temperatures over 100 degrees and with a rationed water supply. They were required to read his pamphlet about tropical warfare while they were on the ship. Consequently, American prisoners were also jammed into freight cars and into the holds of ships.

Other factors contributed to our harsh treatment by the Japanese guards. When Bataan fell, the Japanese had not expected to capture so many prisoners because MacArthur had claimed that the Americans were outnumbered. The Japanese also had not realized how seriously ill, how near starvation, the American troops were.

Furthermore, Colonel Tsuji, in his hatred of the colonial whites and of orientals who helped them, told the field commanders to kill their prisoners. The Filipino officers and noncoms of the 91st Division were massacred. Some Japanese officers refused to obey that command. Colonel Imai, later Lieutenant General of the Japanese home forces during the Korean War, believed that killing prisoners was a violation of a soldier's honor. He remembered the excellent treatment of Russian prisoners under an earlier emperor in the Russo-Japanese War. He told his American and Filipino prisoners to hide in the jungle and mountains until he could guarantee their safety. So Grover Bumps of the army air corps spent two weeks wandering north until he fell in with a column of Filipino and American prisoners near San Fernando.

Another negative factor was the prewar attitude in the United States. Our assistance to the Japanese after the earthquake in 1923 had greatly enhanced U.S. and Japanese relations. But the American immigration law of 1924, the so-called Asiatic Exclusion Act, caused bitterness and anger. The continual cries of "yellow peril" were countered by Japanese propaganda against the "white peril," colonial policies for treating Asia and Asians. Thus the hostility of the Japanese toward their American war prisoners was related to our own racist policies. We, as prisoners, reaped the harvest.

18

ATTENTION

*D*URING THE PREWAR YEARS military training in the United States was a little different from the Japanese system.

On the blustery snowy morning of April 14, 1941, Easter Monday, 77 drafted men were inducted into the U.S. Army at Fort Snelling, Minnesota. Quite a few of us had hangovers from the long Easter weekend. We stripped and passed before a line of bored doctors. As we shuffled forward, we felt very naked and a bit cold.

Behind me came Thomas Steven Joyce. He was missing his four upper front teeth and, like many Depression kids, had no money for dental work. When the doctor okayed him, Steve said, "Look at my teeth, Doc."

The doctor quipped, "What are you going to do—bite the enemy?"

Steve said, "Look at my feet. I'm flat-footed."

The doctor fished out a rubber stamp, printed "Medics" on Steve's form, and said, "Next."

All through the Bataan campaign Steve served as a medic and a stretcher bearer with tireless courage, exposing himself to Japanese fire and walking endless miles on his flat feet. In prison camp he showed the same devotion, risking himself to find clothing for other prisoners and to scrounge for medicine for his friends. He died on a prison ship, still caring for the sick.

On that first day, after the medical reception line, we were thrown uniforms, the 1918 issue, tight around the legs, with buttoned collars, and made of olive-drab wool, scratchy and smelling faintly of mothballs. I was with Harold "Snuffy" Kurvers, Roland "Rocky" Zweber, and Harold Van Alstyne, who would become lifelong friends of mine. When Rocky pointed out that the uniforms didn't fit, the quartermaster said, "See your tailor." We collected outside the building, heckling one another. One of the shortest men in the group, Herman

84

Omansky, was wrapped in his olive-drab overcoat with his hands and feet hidden. He looked around grinning and spotted one of the tallest men, Phil Brain, in a small coat with the cuffs halfway to his elbows. Without a word the two men exchanged coats, and they looked around in triumph, as we stood there with the snow falling gently on us.

The only item of clothing that the army insisted fit perfectly was shoes. I was told to put on the shoes and pick up a pail of sand in each hand. Then the quartermaster corporal checked carefully to see that I had the correct fit.

With First Sergeant Christie, the very model of an old-line first sergeant, everything had to be done by the book. He even ate at attention, watching us out of the corner of his eye, ready to bellow at us for any sign of untoward behavior. When Bill McKeon moved a trunk into our temporary barracks, suddenly there was Sergeant Christie, his barrel chest covered with decorations and his cold eyes aimed at Bill, who was hanging up several civilian suits on the hooks behind his bunk. In an icy but conversational tone Sergeant Christie said to Bill, "I think you presume you're going to the seashore," and then in a roar, "Get that trunk out of here!"

Sergeant Christie ordered us to make our beds in the army way, with square corners and tight enough to bounce a coin. He left while we struggled with it. When he returned, he looked at the nearest bed, Bill Lemke's. The blanket flew one way, the sheet the other, and Sergeant Christie leveled a finger at the bed and blared at Lemke, "What do you think I'm running here, a boar's nest?"

Two and a half days later we boarded a train for the west coast. Now privates at $21 a month in the U.S. Army, we were assigned to something called the 194th Tank Battalion in Fort Lewis, Washington. For this trip we were under another old-time army sergeant, Sergeant Scott, a fine man without rancor or the ribaldry of some of the old army men. The day before we left, some of us worked on a detail fitting up a field kitchen in a railroad baggage car backed onto a spur line on the post. We found ourselves helping Sergeant Scott because he was so low-key, so quietly competent. We helped him muscle a field stove into the empty baggage car. Then he had us build around the stove a square enclosure of two-by-six boards, which he filled with fine white sand from the nearby Mississippi River bank.

The next day we boarded a coach coupled to the baggage-car

Colonel Ernest B. Miller, commander of the 194th Tank Battalion, as a major, Fort Lewis, Washington, 1941. Photo courtesy of Patricia Miller Horner.

kitchen, and after being switched around for a while, we became part of a troop train, with some cars for civilian passengers as well, and we began the long train ride across the country. We thought we would be back home in a year. We spent our time working for Sergeant Scott in the baggage-car kitchen, playing cards, getting to know one another.

Bernard FitzPatrick at Fort Lewis, Washington, shortly after being drafted, May 1941.

As the monotony of the train ride grew, we slept and napped on the hard coach seats. Porters came through now and then and passed out soda pop and fruit. Small towns, snow-covered fields, and mountains appeared and fell behind us down the endless track.

On Saturday, April 20th, the train pulled into a base army depot at Fort Lewis, Washington. Coming from the cold and slushy Minnesota April, we were delighted to see flowers and neatly mown grass. We were shepherded into a line of six-by-six trucks for the short ride to the 194th Tank Battalion area, with relatively new wooden barracks and equipment buildings amid plots of grass and immaculate company streets. We lined up awkwardly with our civilian white duffel bags in front of battalion headquarters. A lean captain in a perfectly fitting uniform, with his shoes and brass sparkling, looked us over with no expression on his face. He turned and went into the headquarters building.

A few seconds later he came out, holding the door for a slightly shorter and heavier officer. He too looked at us. He spoke briefly to the captain and then walked a few steps forward, stood at relaxed attention, and said that he was our commanding officer, Major Miller. "We are glad to have you with us," he said, and after a few more welcoming words, he turned us over to Captain Canby, the battalion executive officer, who assigned us to barracks and ordered us to stay in the battalion area for some inoculations.

Years later Colonel Miller told me how shocked he and Captain Canby had been at our ragtag appearance. The new light tan army shoes, not yet darkened with dubbing and polish, looked oversize with the tight 1918 pants. On Monday morning the battalion supply sergeant, David Carlson, issued us completely new uniforms. An army tailor fitted each uniform precisely. Colonel Miller knew that to be a soldier, one first had to look like one and be able to take pride in one's appearance. Also, Fort Lewis had an atmosphere of spit and polish in those days. Any unit commander who didn't pay attention to such ritual would be courting trouble.

19

PRESENT ARMS

RIGHT AFTER RECEIVING our new uniforms we were assigned to first-rate drill sergeants, and for the next two weeks we spent the mornings learning all the time-honored movements of close-order drill. We worked hard, and soon we were ready for a retreat formation at the end of the day. General Dwight D. Eisenhower, writing in *Crusade in Europe* about his own experience at Fort Lewis, comments on the inadequate equipment at that time. What disturbed him most was the "lack of a sense of urgency" and the officers "bogged down in ruts of professional routine," which served as "a shelter from new ideas and troublesome problems." He explains that, in addition to spit and polish and retreat formations and parades, the main emphasis was on "athletics, recreation and entertainment" instead of "serious training." He worked hard to change this inertia.

Major Miller too was working his hardest to provide practical, realistic training. He insisted on classes in scouting and patrolling in the afternoons. Other instructor sergeants taught us to assemble and dismantle the .30-caliber and .50-caliber machine guns and such handguns as the .38-caliber automatic pistol. We had a short period of dry firing, and then everyone, even the cooks, went out to the range to fire the weapons with live ammunition at least twice a week. We had classroom instruction in all the battalion vehicles, especially the half-tracks and tanks. On the tank training grounds everyone drove a tank and fired the turret machine guns. Even though the tanks were the out-of-date Mae West type, with twin turrets and a high silhouette, we were learning what it meant to be a tanker. But Major Miller and Captain Canby had to struggle continually with red tape to provide us with this sort of training.

When the original National Guard companies of the 194th had arrived at Fort Lewis in February 1941, Major Miller had picked some of the key men from his Company A from Brainerd, Minnesota, and ordered the other company commanders to make similar selections from their companies—Company B from St. Joseph, Missouri, and Company C from Salinas, California. Miller sent these men to communication and armorer's schools at Fort Knox, Kentucky. They came back trained as instructors. Major Alexander, a brisk adviser and training officer, arrived from the armored-force headquarters. With this nucleus Major Miller set up his own schools for the battalion. There was even a small class of battalion noncoms in training to become officers.

At the end of the second week in June I found myself and 14 others assigned to the communications school. Every day became an exhaustingly thorough class in map reading, sending and receiving code, and learning how to talk on the voice radio. As soon as one man was well trained in a skill, he was put to work helping train others.

When we came out of our barracks on a cool, clear morning, we could see the glistening peak of Mount Rainier, long before the sun reached us. We went on guard duty, did KP work, and policed the area. Most of all we trained. After retreat parade we played softball or sang, but often we just flopped on our bunks and rested from a crowded day's work. On weekends we had occasional passes into Tacoma, a few miles south, or Seattle, to the north. For a few weeks I sang in the post chapel, partly for pleasure, partly for extra money. Father Babst, the stern military chaplain, recommended me to a church in Tacoma, where I was hired to sing after the August maneuvers. The army pay of $21 a month didn't go very far, even in those days.

We began to feel that we were under the only tough taskmasters at Fort Lewis. None of the other units seemed to be working as hard or as seriously as we were. The men in other units were constantly on duty taking care of flower beds and arranging lines of whitewashed stones beside pathways. These units were up to their ears in spit and polish. Even the post MPs seemed to single us out for special attention. Our greasy tank coveralls were a special target for them. Shoes had to be shined, ties had to be worn, shirts had to be mathematically creased. Despite this hazing, we felt pride in our training and our outfit and a strong respect, despite our griping about the hard work, for our battalion commander, his executive officer, and Major Alexander.

The lights burned most of the night in battalion headquarters. Major Miller and Captain Canby were the best type of citizen soldier.

They were veterans of the Mexican campaign under General Pershing and of the First World War. They both had a sense of urgency. We were all shocked when we heard that Company B, an especially well-trained company, was to be shipped off to Alaska. Major Miller became grimmer, and he bit harder on his cigars and went ahead with the training.

He sent us on road marches. The whole battalion loaded up and moved out. We bivouacked overnight, sleeping in shelter halves and blankets. I soon bought a sleeping bag at the post exchange. We went on alert for three days when Germany invaded Russia. We were set to guard the Boeing aircraft installations at Seattle, when the alert was called off.

In August 1941 we took part in the beginning of the Pacific coast maneuvers. This was a period of continual frustration for Major Miller. The old army policy, reinforced by order of General MacArthur when he was chief of staff, demanded that the tanks be distributed to various infantry regiments. Major Miller knew that the modern use of tanks was in massed spearheads supported by specially trained infantry, the basis for the blitzkrieg in Europe. He could only protest the misuse of his tanks. We took our maneuvers positions, scattered all over the countryside south of Tacoma. My part of Company A was to guard the long wooden bridge over the Columbia River at Longview, Washington. I took cover from a mock air attack and ate blackberries from the bushes I was crouching under.

Almost as soon as we had taken our positions for maneuvers, however, we received orders to return to Fort Lewis. We had five days to prepare to leave for Angel Island in San Francisco. Our time at Fort Lewis was over. Despite all the obstructions to our training, we had learned to move fast, to move together, to set up camp, to dig foxholes, and to sleep anywhere. Major Alexander said that he had never served on a peace-time post without at least a couple of soldiers being court-martialed every week. We had not had a single court-martial in all our time at Fort Lewis.

We said goodbye to the men we knew in Company B, still waiting for their shipping orders to Alaska. We turned over all our equipment to another tank battalion training at Fort Lewis. A few men who lived nearby went on leave. Then we took the train to San Francisco.

On Angel Island at Fort McDowell the army issued us tropical uniforms, gave us more inoculations, and allowed us an evening pass into San Francisco. Some of us ate a huge meal in Chinatown together. We still had no idea how close we were to war. We did not know that all the tanks, half-tracks, jeeps, command cars, and various weapons would be unfamiliar to us. Despite Major Miller's silence about our destination, a slip by a man at Fort Knox reached the press. We were headed for the Philippine Islands. We were the first armored unit ever to leave the United States to go overseas.

20

PARADE REST

OUR TRAINING at Fort Stotsenburg in the Philippines was in sharp contrast to the get-on-with-it toughness of our training at Fort Lewis. The rainy season, blown in on the monsoon winds from the China Sea through most of October and November, was punctuated by steamy hot days of sun. The immense cavalry drill field would dry, and the seasoned 26th Cavalry would hold impressive formations. The horses, sleek and spirited, were disciplined through all the traditional movements of an old-time cavalry regiment. On the polo field two teams played an exciting game before an audience of curious soldiers. The Indian summer of colonialism in the Far East lived on in the Philippines, as well as in Singapore and Hong Kong.

When it rained, we spent much of our time trying to keep our equipment dry. Vehicles were half-covered by tarpaulins and had to be dried out in the brief sunny spells. Major Miller started classes on how to use our new equipment: the tommy guns and the 37-millimeter guns mounted in our fifty-four M-3 light tanks. In crowded tents with the rain pattering on the canvas, these classes could accomplish only so much. We did learn to drive the new tanks, within the tank park. We had no ammunition to fire the guns, not enough gasoline to get the tanks out on the road, and no recuperating oil for the recoil mechanism of the machine guns. In fact, the 194th was not issued any ammunition or recuperating oil until the first day of the war, December 8, 1941 (Philippine time).

Not far from us, the 200th Coast Artillery (converted to Antiaircraft), which had crossed the Pacific on the *President Coolidge* with us, was having the same troubles. No one would give them permission to go out on the range with their weapons. The cowboys from West Texas and New Mexico, the Indians from the Navajo, Taos, and Apache nations, draftees, and long-term National Guard men alike—they too felt

93

the letdown from rough training in the U.S. to this slow-motion existence at Fort Stotsenburg. The commanding officer of the 200th, Colonel Sage, was an able man trying to get his regiment of 2,000 men trained, but he could not get the tracking and range-finding mechanisms for his antiaircraft weapons until the Japanese had attacked.

One of our first major jobs on reaching Fort Stotsenburg was to install shortwave radios in all the M-3 tanks. These radios, not designed for the M-3, were a stopgap measure until the proper equipment could be sent from the United States. We had to remove one of the .30-caliber machine guns to install the radio, leaving a large hole in each tank. Major Miller repeatedly and unsuccessfully requested permission to have the 17th Ordnance Company weld a steel plate over these holes. After December 8 the major ordered the job done on his own authority.

He was engaged in a constant battle with red tape. Every requisition moved down to USAFFE headquarters in Manila on a stream of molasses and then back to Fort Stotsenburg. In early October Major Miller received news that a ship named the *Yaka* would bring him a large supply of spare parts for all his vehicles. About the middle of October it docked at Manila. From then until war broke out, the major tried to pry those parts out of the Port Area Authority. Eventually, the Japanese captured 13 railroad carloads of M-3 tank parts. And we wondered why his face became grimmer and his cheroot was clamped so hard in his jaw. Through the Chinese tailors at the post exchange Major Miller arranged for some Filipino women to embroider a yellow silk emblem of a tank on all our overseas caps. He pretended that this insignia was regulation back in the United States. For us it was a great morale booster.

On the weekend of October 11 and 12 I had a pass to Manila. I went alone and stayed at the Bay View, the usual hotel in those days for American army men. The good and inexpensive food and the tall, cool gin and tonics in the courtyard of the hotel were very welcome. The weather was mild and sunny. The fountains played in the courtyard, where small palm trees and flowerpots stood about the tables. On Saturday I lingered in the courtyard until dusk, watching through the tall iron grillwork of the Spanish gate the automobiles, trucks, carts, calesas—the two-wheeled carriages painted bright yellow and red and pulled by small horses with resplendent harnesses—and Filipino, American, Chinese, and Japanese pedestrians.

Early Sunday morning I found a calesa outside the hotel and asked the driver where I might go to church. He suggested the church of the sixteenth-century fortress monastery of San Augustine, because they were celebrating the Festival of the Holy Rosary there. "It is a most beautiful service, sir." I climbed in, and he drove his little horse down toward the harbor, across the river, through the thick walls, into the Intramuros, the old walled city, and to the wonderfully ornate entrance of the church of San Augustine. Before mass the statue of the Virgin was carried around the interior of the church in a procession solemn and yet full of the fiesta spirit. It was, indeed, a most beautiful service in honor of Our Lady of the Rosary, San Rosaria, who is especially venerated in the Philippines.

After the mass I walked around to see the cloisters and the monastery. They were closed, but being a curious American, I knocked at the small door set in the huge gates. These gates were built to admit mounted cavalry to the monastery courtyard and stables. After a considerable while the dark whiskered face of a young priest appeared in the door's barred window. "What can I do for you, my son?"

I said that I had hoped to see the monastery. At first he did not want to admit me. He asked for proof that I wasn't British! I told him that I was an American soldier. In those days we did not wear a uniform on pass, just ordinary civilian clothes with a white shirt. When I said my name was FitzPatrick, he promptly opened the door. "With a name like that, you can't be British. Who's going to win the World Series—the Yankees or the Dodgers?"

He had been to Villanova University, had played shortstop for the varsity baseball team, and was delighted to talk to someone who had recently come from the States. He led me across the courtyard cobblestones to the cloisters and refectory. Next he showed me the great hall of the monastery, where the peace treaty between Spain and the United States had been signed in 1898, transferring the Philippines to the United States.

Then he took me back into the church, now empty. He led me behind the altar, pulled aside an embroidered wall hanging, and pointed to a bronze plaque bolted to the stone. I knew just enough Spanish and Latin to read the inscription, recording the formal ecclesiastical malediction against the British. During the Seven Years' War, the British had seized Cuba and the Philippines. From 1761 to 1763 General Draper had occupied Manila and sacked it. Searching for gold, the soldiers had dug up and disturbed some of the chancel burial places of the early conquistadores and churchmen. The abbot at that time had had the plaque inscribed and bolted to the wall.

This young priest guided me through the art treasures and took me down into the crypt, from which led long passages cut into solid rock. Here the Japanese naval forces were to make their last stand when the American invasion returned to Manila in 1945.

I thanked the priest and told him that I hoped the Dodgers would win the World Series but that I thought the Yankees, with Joe DiMaggio, were too strong for them. He beamed and shook hands with me in farewell. I left San Augustine impressed by its age and beauty. For me the Philippines had begun to be a real country that day.

21

AT EASE

*F*OR THE WEEKEND of the Feast of All Hallows, I and some other men from the 194th went on pass to Manila on Friday, October 31. In the late afternoon, just after a fine, soft rain, I met a friend and classmate from the College of St. Thomas, Lieutenant Jim Daly, and we enjoyed frosted rum drinks in the courtyard of the Bay View Hotel. A fellow officer was with him, and we had an excellent dinner in the courtyard, with Spanish and American music played by a string orchestra. After dinner Jim suggested that we take a calesa to a cemetery. I thought it was a joke, but I was the newcomer, and both Jim and his friend were enthusiastic.

That All Hallows festival was a combination of Spanish and Chinese festivals. The whole cemetery was lit with Chinese lanterns. Families prayed at some graves, and children ran to and fro with balloons. In one of the open spaces a cockfight was in progress with loud shouts of encouragement from the bettors, and a noisy dice game was thriving a few feet from a large, well-tended monument. Filipino women dressed in the mestiza costumes, with butterfly sleeves and with mantillas over their hair, strolled among the graves and stopped to pray. They were accompanied by men in barong Tagalog shirts, a semiformal jacket shirt. I was delighted and could have stayed and watched all night, but Jim and his friend decided that I ought to be taken to the Santa Ana Cabaret.

After another short calesa ride we entered what was reputed to be the largest nightclub in the world. As we went in, an attendant rented us formal jackets. We must have received the last evening jackets in stock: mine fit, but Jim had to roll up the sleeves of his. Jim told me the protocol. We had to ask the duennas for permission to dance with the young ladies. As we danced, I told a young lady that I was a corporal stationed at Fort Stotsenburg. She gave me a lingering but regretful smile and said, "How can you speak of love when you are only a cor-poral?" Soon I stopped Jim and introduced him as a lieutenant. Jim and I traded partners.

Jim showed me a special section roped off for General Wainwright and his staff and other high-ranking army and navy officers. I thought it odd that the whole staff from Fort Stotsenburg had time for evenings in Manila. Jim, whose college major had been engineering, talked about his frustrated efforts to prepare Bataan as a defensive strong-hold. "They ought to extend the road on the China Sea side clear up to Olongapo, the naval station and airfield up there. But when I sug-gested that, I was told to relax and do what I was told."

"I think Major Miller in our outfit is getting the same treatment," I said. "He keeps asking for gas and parts and permission to go out on road marches, to get our tanks moving, and I guess the only answers he gets are 'Mañana' and 'No.'"

"Some units quit work at noon most of the time," Jim exploded. "They sent all the wives and dependents back to the States in April. But damn little else has been done."

Late the next morning I called another college friend, Lieutenant Bill Tooley, and we spent a long afternoon in the Bay View Hotel courtyard, reminiscing about the College of St. Thomas and our families back in Minnesota and talking about what we were doing in the Philippines. When I mentioned that there didn't seem to be any concern about war between the United States and Japan, Bill hesitated and looked carefully around him.

"Bernie," he said, "that's what worries me. No one, even at USAFFE, seems concerned at all. My outfit, the 31st Infantry, is sup-posed to be one of the crack regiments of the Philippine Division. The 45th, that Jim Daly's with, and the 57th are the other two regiments. I've hardly seen them. We haven't functioned as a division since I got here. Even the regimental staffs don't know each other. Then there's the Philippine army. They're not even partially mobilized."

I told him what Jim had said the previous evening. Bill cleared a place on the table in front of him. "Look," he said, "the Japanese navy and air force have got us surrounded." He placed some small pineapple leaves in a curve. "Here are the Mandated Islands—the Marianas and so forth that the Japanese got from the Germans after the World War—to the east of us." He nudged a sugar bowl into position. "Up here to the north is Formosa." He lined up some glasses. "And to the west is the China Coast, which is under Japanese control." He put his fist on the table in front of him. "And down here to the southwest is Indochina, where they've just walked in and made themselves at home."

I nodded and said, "How good are they, Bill?"

"They're tough, Bernie. They've been going to school over there in China. And every time I realize that this wet season is just about over, I get to thinking that it's the ideal time for them to attack." He took another look around and leaned over to me. "We get the word that MacArthur and his people at USAFFE think they won't come at us until April, if at all. Why would they wait around for the monsoon and the rains to start again? You tell me!"

Major Miller's efforts to speed up the training of the battalion began to succeed about the beginning of November. The gasoline he had requested, in good supply right at Fort Stotsenburg, was released to the 194th. He was allowed to send small reconnaissance missions to circle the area around Fort Stotsenburg and Clark Field. After each mission he submitted map overlays to General King, as both a report and a help to build up the maps of the area. Gradually, the 194th began to do some useful training.

Then, to Major Miller's surprise, he was granted permission to make an overnight march to Lingayen Gulf, about 70 miles north of Fort Stotsenburg. Immediately, the 194th went into high gear. Except for a few guards, every man and every vehicle moved out. Company commanders watched for places to put up roadblocks. Tank drivers were told to remember every inch of the road. We crossed the Agno River, where we would later hold the line against the advancing Japanese at Christmas, and we came out on one of the longest and most beautiful beaches I have ever seen. Somewhere close to Lingayen, the sleepy capital of Pangasinan province, we bivouacked for the night, after we had cooled off in the shallows of the gulf. On the way back Major Miller took as much of an alternate route as was possible. That was our only full-scale march before the Japanese attack three weeks later.

We all looked forward to that first Thanksgiving away from home, on November 20, 1941, and the cooks put in a lot of overtime. Most of our food was canned, but for this occasion the turkeys had been shipped all the way from the United States. We had just sat down to eat that Thanksgiving dinner when most of the battalion was rousted out to make ready for the arrival of a new tank battalion, the 192nd, and Company D from Harrodsburg, Kentucky, which was to join the 194th. Company D had an intelligent, coolheaded, and hardworking commanding officer, Captain Jack Altman. On the same ship with them was a full colonel, James Weaver, a graduate of West Point, to become the commanding officer of the First Tank Group, composed of the 194th and the 192nd. Colonel Weaver, soon to be promoted to brigadier general by USAFFE, had only the sketchiest knowledge of the capabilities and limitations of a tank.

As late as the third weekend in November we made a joyous sightseeing trip. Perhaps 50 of us rolled out of Fort Stotsenburg at noon on a Saturday in battalion six-by-six trucks and headed down Route 3 to Manila. The Bay View Hotel stuffed us with good food and the light Filipino beer. Early Sunday morning we left in pambuscos to see the waterfall on the Pagsanjan River, about 65 miles east and south of Manila. The pambusco drivers took the northern route around Laguna de Bay, the great volcanic lake. The road was narrow and unsurfaced. About a dozen miles out of Manila the road climbed along the edge of the mountains above Laguna de Bay. The dust billowed up behind us as we jounced around sharp corners with no guardrails and with steep drops of hundreds of feet. The pambusco driver calmly drew on his long, thin dobie cigarette and stepped on the gas.

The pambusco took us to the bridge crossing the river just below the falls. Some of the men went for a swim, and others went with Filipino boatmen to paddle out to the spray below the falls and run the rapids under the bridge and on down the river. Bill McKeon and I looked at the dugout canoes and decided to watch from the bridge. The sun was hot and a cool, wet breeze came from the falls. Bill's pith helmet fell into the river, and he shouted loudly for someone to rescue it. A Filipino boy made a dash and missed it. Bill solemnly pulled out his side arm and shot the helmet as it floated away. Wet and tired and happy, we piled into the pambusco and returned by the better road along the south shore of Laguna de Bay, to arrive back at Fort Stotsenburg about midnight. We had seen some of the Philippine countryside that we were not allowed to see from our tanks and half-tracks.

We had a few more days of training with our new company. The quartermaster at Fort Stotsenburg tried to take over the ten-ton wrecker. Major Miller skillfully got the ordnance department to explain the necessity of the wrecker to the tank battalion. But we were not so lucky with a requisition from MacArthur's headquarters. Nine days before the start of the war, some of our jeeps, reconnaissance cars, and trucks were ordered to be sent to the port quartermaster in Manila. Major Miller's protests were brushed aside. When the vehicles arrived in Manila, no one was there to receive them: the responsible officer was taking his afternoon siesta.

Major Miller had an official plan for the 194th in case of an alert. Colonel Lester Maitland, in charge of Clark Field, and Colonel Sage of the 200th Antiaircraft, had initiated the plan and had agreed to Major Miller's suggestions. Major Miller had arranged for a conference with the Fort Stotsenburg intelligence officer, Lieutenant Colonel Charles E. Lainbach, to coordinate reconnaissance and map information. Captain Spoor, the battalion intelligence officer, reported to Major Miller that Colonel Lainbach had told him that the 194th was going to a lot of "unnecessary work, because it would be absolutely impossible for the Japanese to attack the Philippines successfully."

On December 1, 1941, we went on alert. For the next week we stood by our tanks in the cogon grass beside Clark Field, to repel a possible paratroop landing with no ammunition for the tanks and with no recuperating oil for the 37-millimeter guns. Only the tommy guns and our side arms were ready to shoot. That week the *Manila Times* and the Manila radio station KZRH carried General MacArthur's denial that there was an alert. We had all heard from officers about MacArthur's theory that the Japanese would not attack until April 1942 and that the Japanese were so bogged down in China that they couldn't possibly attack the Philippines.

Clark Field had more modern planes than in Hawaii or on any other U.S. air base. The disaster of Clark Field was obscured in the flames of Pearl Harbor. Distance and difficulty of communications kept many Americans unaware of the devastating Japanese attack on the Philippines, even though MacArthur had a warning of nine hours.

22

TO MEASURE THE STRENGTH

I N THE MONTHS before the outbreak of war and during the months of fighting in the Philippines until he fled to Australia—months of poor planning and fatal vacillation—General Douglas MacArthur seemed to function in a daze. But when he sailed for the Philippines in the fall of 1935 to begin as military adviser to the Philippine government, he was the American military officer reputed to know the most about the Orient in general and the Philippines in particular. He had served four tours of duty in the Philippines, with side trips to other parts of the Far East. In 1905 he had taken an extraordinary journey with his father, Major General Arthur MacArthur, to inspect first the Japanese army and navy at the end of the Russo-Japanese war and then to observe and report on Japan, Southeast Asia, and India in a luxurious grand tour of the Far East.

In his *Reminiscences* Douglas MacArthur writes, "The purpose of our observations was to measure the strength of the Japanese Army and its methods of warfare." He expresses respect and admiration for the Japanese soldier's dedication, staying power, and capabilities as a fighting man. One lesson of the Russo-Japanese war was that the Japanese had attacked Russia without a warning, without a declaration of war. In 1922, when the war-plans division in Washington formulated War Plan Orange—a contingency plan for the defense of the Philippines—its basic premise was that the Japanese would attack without warning at the beginning of the dry season, in December or January.

The focus of MacArthur's four tours of duty in the Philippines repeatedly included the defenses of Manila Bay: Corregidor, its attendant islands, and Bataan. Even on his first, brief tour of duty in 1903, fresh out of West Point, one of his main jobs was "harbor improvement in Manila Bay, fortification installations of Corregidor, traverses over the steaming wooded hills of Bataan."

After his meteoric rise to the rank of brigadier general in the Rainbow Division in the First World War, MacArthur became superintendent of West Point at the permanent rank of brigadier general. Here he spent three years modernizing the educational system, with considerable intelligence and against stubborn opposition. Then in October 1922 he returned to the Philippines for his second tour of duty.

In the leisurely colonial atmosphere of those days, MacArthur had time for a pleasant social life, beyond the formal arrangements of the military and naval personnel and the politically important parties given by the governor-general, Leonard Wood. MacArthur renewed his friendship with the Philippine president, Manuel Quezon, whom he had met as a student in 1904, and soon he was on close terms with many of the upper-class Filipino families. His association with these Filipino leaders was resented by Americans in the business and military establishments. MacArthur's attitudes toward the Filipino people were always colored by his association with the Filipino leaders, whose sense of superiority was based on their Spanish traditions and their education at the University of Santo Tomás.

In June 1923 MacArthur was given command of the 23rd Brigade of the Philippine Division, which included the 45th and 57th regiments of the Philippine Scouts. Under General Omar Bundy this division was used to help control livestock epidemics, to back up the Philippine constabulary against bandits, and to train ROTC officers for the recently established University of the Philippines. MacArthur was also ordered, according to his *Reminiscences*,

> to make a thorough study of Bataan, and to draw up a plan of defense for this mountainous and wooded peninsula lying a scant three miles across the sea channel from the island of Corregidor, at the mouth of Manila Bay. In the ensuing weeks I covered every foot of rugged terrain, over its trails, up and down its steep mountainous slopes, and through its bamboo thickets.

During the dry season from November 1923 through April 1924, MacArthur's engineers mapped 40 square miles of Bataan, about one-tenth of the peninsula, which in total is 30 miles long by about 14 miles wide. The survey was continued by the chief engineer of the Philippine department. MacArthur knew part of Bataan well, but he did not know "every foot." If he had continued to command that mapping survey, he might have learned that trails hacked out of the jungle in one dry season were grown over by the next dry season. In two wet seasons the jungle obliterated even the signs of a trail.

Shortly after a nonviolent mutiny among the Philippine Scouts in July 1924, MacArthur was given command of the Philippine Division. He was known for believing in equal treatment of Filipino and American soldiers. In January 1925 he received his promotion to the permanent rank of major general. The War Department ordered him back to the United States in the summer of 1925. He served with meticulous attention to his duties as commanding general of the Third Corps Area, with his headquarters in Baltimore.

MacArthur returned to the Philippines in the fall of 1928. During this third tour of duty there he was in command of all the troops in the Philippines. The chief directive from the War Department to MacArthur has a familiar ring to it: "Every preparation will be made in these fortifications [defending the entrance to Manila Bay] to withhold a protracted siege."

On November 21, 1930, President Hoover appointed MacArthur chief of staff, and for five long years through the Depression the general fought a rearguard action in Washington against sharply curtailed military spending, cuts in every phase of the military establishment, which was already nearly impotent from the wave of pacifism in the 1920s and 1930s.

When President Quezon requested that MacArthur become military adviser to the Philippine government until the Philippines became independent from America, MacArthur was given a perfect alternative to stepping down from the pinnacle of chief of staff and retiring into oblivion. In the fall of 1935 he returned to the Philippines. Two years later he resigned his commission in the U.S. Army and accepted the title of Field Marshal of the Philippines. In his *Reminiscences* he explains, "I was under two masters, one the American Government, and the other the Philippine Government. The growing coolness between Roosevelt and Quezon made my position almost untenable."

Because MacArthur had resigned from the U.S. Army, he no longer had direct chain-of-command relations with the War Department in Washington or with the Philippine department commander, nor did he have a clear interservice relationship with the American naval commander, Admiral Thomas C. Hart. His highly paid station as field marshal and his constant political relationships with Quezon and the Philippine Commonwealth government put him in an awkward position with these officers. His showy, self-designed uniform with the famous "scrambled-egg" hat and the expensive penthouse apartment atop the Manila Hotel were theatrical staging for MacArthur. They were taken for granted by his staff, but they were an affront to the more austere army and navy men.

In letters to Washington, MacArthur was angling for the job of head of the American forces in the Far East. In April 1941 he wrote again to President Roosevelt's secretary, Stephen Early, to announce that he was about to terminate his mission as military adviser and move back to San Antonio, Texas. He even booked reservations for himself and his family on a passenger ship. As he made these maneuvers, he knew that the Philippine army would soon be mobilized. In July 1941 he was called back into the service to command all United States Armed Forces in the Far East (USAFFE). At the same time the Philippine army, air force, and navy were inducted into the armed forces of the United States. MacArthur was supreme commander.

MacArthur's knowledge of the Japanese was seriously inadequate. For a long time he thought that they would not attack at all because they were bogged down in China and had neither the men nor the resources to invade the Philippines. Then, in the face of warnings from Washington and Joseph Grew, our ambassador to Japan, MacArthur convinced himself that the Japanese would not attack before April 1942. Why he thought the Japanese would have been so foolish as to attack near the beginning of the wet season remains a mystery.

MacArthur also overestimated the capability of the Filipino-American forces to resist invasion. And he misjudged the possibilities of relief to be provided by the American navy, even before the debacle at Pearl Harbor. At the time of the attack on Pearl Harbor, Japan had at least ten carriers, whereas we had only three in the Pacific. The standard navy fighter for the Japanese was the Zero, proven in combat and faster than the comparable German, British, or American planes.

Before the attack MacArthur bred optimism both in the Philippines and in Washington. Writing to Miguel Elizalde, the Philippine resident commissioner in Washington, he accused the American press, particularly *Time* magazine, of underestimating "the fighting capacity of the Philippine Army." John Hersey interviewed MacArthur in May 1941 and came away with the conviction that the combined Allied forces in the Far East "could handle [Japan] with about half the forces they now have." MacArthur told Hersey that Japan was in trouble in China and that "twelve Filipino divisions are already trained."

MacArthur optimistically abandoned the defensive War Plan Orange and embarked on his own overconfident scheme of meeting the Japanese invasion "on the beaches." MacArthur seems not to have thought through any contingency plan in case the meeting on the beaches failed. He dissipated fuel, food, and munitions by establishing forward depots at Tarlac, Los Banos, Cabanatuan, and elsewhere. Ammunition even accumulated at Dagupan, on the Lingayen Gulf. These depots were only partially evacuated before the Japanese captured them. As of February 20, 1942, the Japanese 14th Army had captured 4 million gallons of fuel, about 70 artillery pieces, and many rifles.

Once the war had begun, MacArthur again exaggerated his situation to the opposite extreme. By his insistence that the Japanese had a huge advantage in combat troops, air power, and supplies, he led Washington to a pessimistic view. During the entire Luzon campaign the Japanese 14th Army never exceeded 60,000 men, of whom only half were combat troops. But in a communiqué dated December 24, 1941, MacArthur claimed that 80,000 Japanese combat troops had landed at Lingayen alone. He apparently thought that the Japanese had six divisions instead of two. In his *Reminiscences* he says, "This was about twice my own strength on Luzon." In fact, the reverse was true: General Homma had half the number of MacArthur's forces, although many Filipino soldiers remained virtually untrained and had never fired their rifles.

When MacArthur declared Manila an open city on December 26, 1941, his purpose was admirable: to halt the bombing of civilians, for whom no bomb shelters had been prepared. Nevertheless, his announcement continued, "in order that no excuse may be given for a possible mistake, the American High Commissioner, the Commonwealth Government, and all combatant military installations will be withdrawn from its environs as rapidly as possible." During the next five days, however, General Albert M. Jones's Southern Luzon Force was still hastening through the city toward Bataan, and MacArthur's deputy chief of staff, Brigadier General Richard J. Marshall, and the quartermaster department were still evacuating supplies that MacArthur should have ordered moved two weeks earlier. Lieutenant Malcolm Champlin finally burned the commercial stores of petroleum products to prevent their falling into Japanese hands. The last of MacArthur's forces left Manila helter-skelter late on New Year's Eve. Not actually an open city during the five days December 27–31, Manila was still the scene of intense military activity.

During the trial of General Homma in 1946, Homma's American attorneys moved to dismiss the charge of violating this open-city declaration by continuing to bomb Manila. MacArthur insisted on retaining the charge. General Homma had shown restraint in his seizure of Manila. His troops waited outside the city for a full day, and then on January 2 Homma allowed only one battalion from the northern force and one from the southern force to march into the city. They had strict orders not to loot or bother civilians.

23

I SHALL RETURN

THE PRIMARY PURPOSES of War Plan Orange were to deny the enemy the use of Manila Bay and its fine anchorage and to provide a bastion for American and Filipino troops. A complex mine field and the heavy guns on Corregidor and its companion fortified islands made the bay impregnable to a naval assault. Manila Bay could be secured only by capturing Bataan and then shelling Corregidor into submission.

First, according to War Plan Orange, the civilians living on Bataan were to be evacuated. Then up to 20,000 laborers were to be hired to build fortifications and tunnels to hide supplies. Sufficient food, medicine, ammunition, and other material were to be stocked to last 40,000 men for six months. Bataan's jungle-covered mountainous terrain was ideal for the type of defense that the Japanese later brought to a fine art on Iwo Jima and Okinawa.

The troops moving into Bataan in the last days of 1941 and the first week of January 1942 knew about War Plan Orange and thought they were retreating into prepared positions, well fortified and amply supplied with food, medicine, and clothing. Nurses went to Bataan certain that hospitals were already established. Sergeant Burt Ellis of the 31st Infantry Regiment observed the hurried departure from the barracks at Cuartel d'España in the Intramuros section of Manila. In charge of the last truck to leave, Burt didn't worry about loading up extra food because he had been told everything was there. His only concern was to pull out and be across the Calumpit bridges before they were blown.

The first stroke of disillusionment came in the early days of January, when MacArthur reduced the 80,000 soldiers on Bataan to half rations. The term *half ration* is deceptive. As General Jonathan Wainwright explains in *General Wainwright's Story*, it meant half of a Filipino ration. Canned fish and rice were substituted for meat and wheat. The new bill of fare was closer to one-third of a normal American army ration. In March there was a further cut of one-third. For the last month the soldiers on Bataan lived on about half a meal a day, when they could get that much. Toward the end many of them were not fed at all.

Ten million tons of rice were stored at Cabanatuan. Because of a law that forbade the transportation of rice from one province to another, some writers have excused MacArthur for not moving this rice to Bataan, and other writers have claimed that there was insufficient transportation. But on August 19, 1941, the National Assembly gave President Quezon the power "to take over solely for use or operation by the government during the existence of the emergency, any public service or enterprise." Furthermore, the Philippine government had not yet been granted its independence from the United States, so when war was declared, MacArthur, as head of USAFFE, had the authority to take almost any step he wished. Nevertheless, he never granted permission to move the rice from Cabanatuan, although boxcars stood idle there for two weeks after the Japanese attack on December 8. The railroad could have taken the rice all the way to Guagua, on the outskirts of Bataan.

Food was not all that was in short supply. Mosquito nets and quinine, to combat the anopheles mosquito and the malaria parasite it carries, are vital in Bataan. There were few nets, and the quinine soon ran out, except for the small supplies a few doctors brought. As the Americans were forced deeper into Bataan, particularly into the low-lying areas of the peninsula, malaria became an omnipresent illness. The Japanese also suffered from it, but they were better fed.

The near paralysis of will at USAFFE headquarters perhaps resulted from three causes. First, MacArthur's own plan to defend the entire Philippine Islands required abandoning War Plan Orange, which he condemned as "defeatist." But then MacArthur's widely scattered troops and supply depots were difficult to reassemble when MacArthur reverted to the War Plan Orange strategy of concentrating forces in Bataan. To admit error was nearly impossible for MacArthur, and he could not bring himself to execute the renewed War Plan Orange wholeheartedly.

Second, Quezon held out an illusory possibility for MacArthur to escape the trap. Quezon wanted independence for the Philippines without paying the price of making the islands militarily self-sufficient.

In May 1939, without a word to MacArthur, Quezon went to Japan and attempted to secure a neutral status for the Philippines. He blandly told the newspapers that these meetings were for "economic purposes." When MacArthur failed to protect Clark Field during the hours after the attack on Pearl Harbor, he was perhaps counting on some agreement about neutrality. When the first few hours of the war were upon him, he seems to have believed that if he committed no aggressive act, the Japanese might not strike at the Philippines. Later, on February 8, 1942, Quezon sent a message to President Roosevelt to suggest that the Philippines be granted independence and then become neutral, with the Americans withdrawing and the Philippine army disbanding. MacArthur sent his own note explaining that his men were "nearly done" and that Quezon's plan "might offer the best possible solution of what is about to be a disastrous debacle."

The third probable cause of MacArthur's inaction is reminiscent of the imaginary land of Laputa in Jonathan Swift's *Gulliver's Travels*. The rulers of Laputa live on an island that floats in the sky. These rulers create grandiose schemes and order them initiated, and then their attention wanders to new schemes. The people on the land below face the practical problems and bear the expense of their irrelevant government in the sky. MacArthur's staff had only one West Pointer, Hugh Casey, MacArthur's chief of engineers. No other army commander in the Second World War had a staff with a similar paucity of West Point officers. MacArthur's "Bataan Gang" was composed mainly of officers who owed MacArthur for their sudden promotion to high rank. They insulated MacArthur from the outside world. With the Japanese forces advancing south toward Manila, commanders in the field tried to phone MacArthur at USAFFE headquarters and were told by the chief of staff, General Richard K. Sutherland, that "the general cannot be disturbed" or "the general will make that decision." General Wainwright once suggested an immediate attack, but one of MacArthur's aides-de-camp, Colonel Constant Irwin, told him, "Submit your plan in triplicate." When officers did succeed in seeing MacArthur, it was to listen, not to suggest or question.

With Olympian detachment MacArthur and his staff issued confused orders and erroneous communiqués. The USAFFE ordered Colonel Napoleon Boudreau to retreat out of Fort Wint on Grande Island, which was armed, amply supplied, and well manned by marines and coast artillerymen. Boudreau's protests were ignored. Who had initiated the order? No one seemed to know. What were the reasons for the move? No one seemed to know. Why leave the "little Corregidor," which blocked the entrance to Subic Bay and covered the western flank of Bataan and the docks of Olongapo? No one seemed to know and no one wished to talk about it. Fort Wint was evacuated, and the Japanese later seized it without a shot.

One of the most crucial periods of the retreat into Bataan was the defense of the Calumpit bridges, allowing the South Luzon Force under General Jones to proceed to Bataan. At that time General Wainwright had received the 91st Division to bolster his defenses, but he was ordered to send the artillery units ahead into Bataan. To hold the main Japanese force coming south down Route 5 toward Manila, Wainwright had a motley assortment of units, none at full strength. Without informing Wainwright, MacArthur's chief of staff, General Sutherland, ordered General Jones to take command of all the forces still on the east bank of the Pampanga River. Before the confusion was resolved, half of the defending force had retreated across the Calumpit bridges as originally ordered. Excellent work by the self-propelled mobile artillery and the 71st Field Artillery and a wild attack by the 192nd tankers kept Plaridel from being overrun. The USAFFE also caused confusion by retaining control of the tanks and the 91st Division and deploying them without coordination with the field commanders.

In his communiqués MacArthur referred to his forces as "greatly outnumbered" and occasionally reported that they had won battles that were actually never fought. After the Clark Field attack and before the Japanese invasion, Carl Mydans, a *Life* reporter, went to Lingayen Gulf to check on MacArthur's press release about an attempted Japanese landing that had been repulsed by a Philippine division. He could find no evidence of a battle there. Pic Diller, MacArthur's press officer, countered Mydans's objections by pointing to his own press release and saying, "It says so here." The *New York Times* for December 14, 1941, carried the headline "Japanese Forces Wiped Out in Western Luzon." MacArthur's communiqués on March 8 and 9 gave a thrilling but incorrect story of General Homma's hara-kiri in MacArthur's former Manila Hotel suite and of the arrival of General Tomoyuki Yamashita as his successor. Homma was alive and did not leave the Philippines until August 1942.

One of MacArthur's most falsified communiqués concerned the Buna-Gona-Santananda Point campaign in New Guinea. He insisted that he had told his commanders not to hurry and to use every precaution to avoid loss of life, and he claimed that the casualties were very light. In actuality, commanders and soldiers had been repeatedly ordered to speed up the fighting, and the casualties among the Australians and the Americans were very heavy. If you served under MacArthur in this campaign, you had a 1 in 11 chance of dying, whereas if you served with the marines on Guadalcanal, you had a 1 in 33 chance of dying.

In his *Reminiscences* MacArthur pictures himself moving through a group of tattered, exhausted, starving soldiers on Bataan:

> Their hoarse, wild laughter greeted the constant stream of obscene and ribald jokes issuing from their parched, dry throats. They cursed the enemy and in the same breath jeered at the Navy. But their eyes would light up and they would cheer when they saw my battered, and much reviled in America, "scrambled-egg" cap. They would gather round and pat me on the back and "Mabuhay Macarsar" me. They would grin—that ghastly skeleton-like grin of the dying—as they would roar in unison, "We are the battling bastards of Bataan—no papa, no mama, no Uncle Sam."

I have never met a soldier from Bataan who had seen MacArthur except on his single brief visit with Wainwright and Parker on January 10, 1942. I have never met a soldier, American or Filipino, who would have thought of patting MacArthur on the back if he *had* seen him. No one called him "Mabuhay Macarsar." One soldier has said to me, "I was too busy hunting for extra food and too damn sick to even think that much about the guy." And soldiers did not jeer at the navy on Bataan. The whole passage is a fantasy of how MacArthur would have liked it to be.

MacArthur was awarded the Congressional Medal of Honor for his defense of Bataan and Corregidor. The citation was written by General George Catlett Marshall, with suggestions from General Sutherland, with concurrence from Secretary of War Henry L. Stimson and President Roosevelt, perhaps partly because they had ordered him to leave Corregidor. Contrary to most of the writing about that epic departure, the starving men on Bataan knew he was on Corregidor, knew he was going to leave, and knew how he was going to leave. They were unimpressed by MacArthur's lingering until the right moment, by his melodramatic departure on a PT boat instead of a submarine, and by his arrival in Australia with the slogan "I shall return."

From Australia, 4,000 miles away, MacArthur insisted upon exercising remote control over the soldiers at Bataan and Corregidor. He was annoyed when Marshall and Roosevelt made General Wainwright head of United States Forces in the Philippines (USFIP), although the USAFFE designation continued with MacArthur's command in Australia. His communiqués became more and more out of touch with the reality of the Philippines. On March 26 Wainwright reported to the War Department that there was only enough food on Bataan to last until April 15, "at one-third ration, poorly balanced and very deficient in vitamins—the troops there will be starved into submission." MacArthur, to whom a copy of the message was sent, wired Marshall that when he had left, there had been enough food to last until May 1, and he added, "It is of course possible that with my departure the rigor of application of conservation may have been relaxed." On April 4, five days before the surrender, MacArthur sent Wainwright a fanciful plan whereby I and II Corps would attack through the Japanese lines and seize the Japanese supplies at Olongapo, 20 miles north of the Pilar-Bagac line, and then fight their way into northern Luzon to continue resistance as guerrillas.

General King took it upon himself to surrender the 80,000 troops on Bataan when the Japanese artillery was close to the two field hospitals, which were crowded with thousands of the sick and wounded. Wainwright, under direct orders from MacArthur, could only order King to attack. Yet in MacArthur's headquarters in Australia—contingent upon MacArthur's approval—was President Roosevelt's message giving Wainwright the freedom to choose his own course of action under the necessities of the battle. Wainwright was furious when, five days after the surrender of Bataan, he received this message with MacArthur's apology for the delay: "I am sorry." Later, when Wainwright, facing the possibility of a slaughter on Corregidor, ordered all the troops in the Philippines to surrender, MacArthur told Marshall that Wainwright had "temporarily become unbalanced."

In *Eagle Against the Sun*, the military historian Ronald H. Spector assesses MacArthur's "muddled planning" and concludes that "the troops on Luzon would have been defeated in any case, but without MacArthur they might have been defeated without being racked by disease and tortured by slow starvation." In May 1942 in O'Donnell

Prison Camp, General William E. Brougher concluded his 11th Division operations report to Wainwright with this paragraph:

> Who had the right to say that 20,000 Americans should be sentenced without their consent and for no fault of their own to an enterprise that would involve for them endless suffering, cruel handicap, death, or a hopeless future that could end only in a Japanese prisoner of war camp in the Philippines? Who took the responsibility for saying that some other possibility was in prospect? And whoever did, was he not an arch-deceiver, traitor and criminal rather than a great soldier? Didn't he know that he was sentencing all his comrades to sure failure, defeat, death, or rotting in a prison camp? A foul trick of deception has been played on a large group of Americans by a commander in chief and small staff who are now eating steak and eggs in Australia. God damn them!

Part Three

IN THE POKEY

24

CAMP O'DONNELL

IN THE EARLY AFTERNOON heat of April 1942 we straggled out of the town of Capas on the hard, dry dirt road. The land stretched out flat on both sides of us—sun-browned cogon grass overrunning fields, the withered stubble of cut rice, a small cemetery with painted saints, a few trees, and an occasional nipa shack where a Filipino family still lived. Beside the road curving past one of these houses, we again saw earthenware crocks and large, square lard cans filled with water. Our guards left us alone—one even held up a weary, sick American— and we could dip out a drink with a canteen cup as we walked by. At another house a Filipino cautiously tossed us small cakes of raw sugar. A bite of one of them hit our starved, dehydrated bodies like a jigger of grain alcohol.

The sun-scorched ground burned through the thin, worn soles of my shoes. How the many men without shoes stood it, I don't know. Finally our strung-out column came to the top of a low ridge, and we could see Camp O'Donnell sprawled out below us. The road led straight through the camp and dipped down to a small river. The land beyond rose gradually to the east and north into the Zambales Mountains, faint and faded blue in heat shimmer. As we came closer we could see the barbed-wire fence and the guard towers and the barracks, called bahays, made of woven bamboo with nipa-palm roofs. Almost nothing moved in that whole camp. We were eager to get out of the sun.

About one-third of the way into the camp, with the barbed wire on each side of the road, we came to the main gate to the smaller part of the camp on our right. Here our guards turned us over to the camp guards, who, yelling "Speedo! Speedo!" herded us up a slight rise to ground trampled bare in front of a one-story wooden building, the Japanese headquarters.

117

Two officers from the 194th, Major Canby and Captain Spoor, and an officer from another outfit quietly walked over to us and told us to get rid of any Japanese money or souvenirs. "The Japanese will accuse you of looting dead Japanese soldiers," Major Canby explained, "and they'll cut your head off if you don't get rid of the stuff. We've been here several days—we know. Take it easy. Don't do it openly."

The Japanese guards searched us at their leisure and left us to stand and wait in the sun. It was still April 17, 1942, eight days after the fall of Bataan. Perhaps thirty minutes passed, an eternity of near sunstroke to us.

Then the Japanese commander, Captain Tsuneyoshi, made his appearance. He wore boots, a sword, and a white shirt open at the neck. He and a uniformed interpreter marched ostentatiously to a small, raised platform. He began screaming at us, working himself into an hysterical state until he was frothing at the mouth. He would rage at us and then step back a bit, and the interpreter would relay the message in English. He told us that we were not prisoners of war: we were horyo, dishonored captives. We would be treated as such until America left the Orient. We were the eternal enemies of Japan. Japan would fight America for 100 years if necessary.

We were so hungry, so dehydrated, so dazed with thirst and fatigue and the heat of the sun, that his ranting had little effect on us. Then suddenly it was over. The captain vanished into headquarters. We were sorted out and taken to different parts of the camp. Major Canby led my group to the corner of the camp near the road, where Colonel Miller saw that we were assigned to bahays occupied by members of the 194th and 192nd Tank battalions. My bahay was partially completed, with a raised bamboo floor to sleep on and a nipa roof to give us shade. I collapsed on my two-foot-wide space between two other prisoners and fell asleep.

The next morning I awoke just before daybreak. I groped in my musette bag, which I had carried all the way from Bataan. I still had my canteen, canteen cup, mess kit, and spoon. When we had surrendered and the battalion's meager remaining supplies had been divided up, I had received some quinine, a few vitamin tablets, a toothbrush and tube of toothpaste, a bar of soap, and a razor and blades. The razor, blades, and mess-kit knife and fork had been looted from me at one of the shakedowns, but I still had everything else. I had never taken my musette bag off my shoulder except for the shakedowns.

"Rules and Regulations," a drawing by Ben Steele.

I had used it as a pillow whenever I got a chance to sleep. Now, thinking I was among friends, I took only my canteen and went to the water line, moving slowly toward one of the two spigots in our American side of the camp. After waiting in line for nearly an hour, I filled my canteen and went back to the bahay in the sudden dawn.

My musette bag was gone. I almost went berserk. I searched through the whole bahay. Other prisoners looked at me with blank faces.

Gradually, the lesson came home to me: I could trust no one. I brooded on that loss for a long time. Until we again were able to help and trust one another, we were truly horyo—war prisoners, criminals, the lowest of the low. We slowly groped our way back to our humane bearings through the next six months.

We seldom left our spaces in the bahays except to eat, get water, and go to the shallow straddle-trench latrines. We did not move unless

"Water Brigade," a drawing by Ben Steele.

we had to or were ordered to. The two spigots gave us barely enough water to drink, so for cooking the strongest men carried water from the stream. The water was muddy and polluted, and we had scarcely enough fuel to boil it for the rice.

Colonel Miller, who gave us the only organization we had at that time, had ordered the straddle trenches dug. Those with dysentery often did not have the strength to reach them, or their uncontrollable bowels would not allow them to reach them in time. Other men, who did not yet have dysentery, would go for days without a bowel movement, because of the shortage of food. Dehydrated as we were, we had a terrible urge to urinate. Sometimes men would black out and fall down when they tried to urinate, and unless someone got them up, they might never have risen again.

Colonel Miller also organized a makeshift kitchen in the center of our bahay. In the large cooking pots called kawalis, we made lugao, a thin rice gruel, and a watery soup with gourds or konkon, a weed that before cooking was so hard and fibrous that prisoners made whistles of it and called it whistleweed. For the soup we occasionally had camote, a vegetable like a sweet potato. Usually, at breakfast we received a small spoonful of raw sugar to flavor the tasteless lugao. And until the end of our years in prison camp we drank tea, green and unsweetened. Men were so suspicious of one another that we took turns doing the cooking.

The Japanese left us alone. Death gradually became familiar. When one got up in the morning, there was usually someone dead nearby. I remember a barracks leader calling out, "Rise and shine. Shake the men on each side of you and see if they're alive." Men standing in the water line sometimes toppled over. Those beside them often took no notice and merely moved up a space. Some men crawled under a bahay to get out of the sun and died there. When the stench became unbearable someone would see that the bodies were removed. The burial detail carried the bodies in shelter halves or blankets slung on a bamboo pole. The bodies were dumped in shallow mass graves outside the camp fence toward the river. By the time I left O'Donnell, bodies were stacked like cordwood beside the bahays. Most of us hardly noticed the stench. Flies and mosquitoes were everywhere. The flies quivered in curtains over the rice, the soup, the feces, and the dead and the living. The mosquitoes brought malaria to the few who had so far escaped it.

Most of the doctors and corpsmen had remained on Bataan in the two field hospitals. The few doctors who had made the Hike were in very poor condition, but they and the corpsmen maintained some buildings as a hospital. In one of these bahays, named St. Peter's Ward, the worst cases were laid side by side on the dirt floor. Little could be done for them, and most died soon. General King asked the Japanese commander that a detail be sent back into Bataan for medical and other supplies. He offered his personal guarantee that no one would attempt to escape or cause any trouble. Captain Tsuneyoshi was said to have replied, "General, you have one job: to look after your dead."

About a week after I entered Camp O'Donnell, the Japanese headquarters ordered us to shave and cut our hair. Two razor blades were issued to each company. Some of the men who had ridden in trucks from Bataan to O'Donnell had not been looted and had razors and scissors. Others, to meet the Japanese deadline, shaved with pieces of broken glass. We cut one another's hair in no special style, just short. Why the Japanese order? To honor the emperor's birthday, April 29! As part of the celebration, we were issued carabao meat, one-

"His Own," a drawing by Ben Steele.

quarter of a carcass per 500 men, enough to make a watery gravy for the rice.

After about ten days my head began to clear, and I looked around more curiously. I learned that Camp O'Donnell had been deserted at the beginning of the war when the 71st Philippine Division had moved out. The barbed wire, a mixture of old and new strands, made a very flimsy fence about ten feet high. The thatching had been blown askew on the neglected bahay roofs, but we had neither the material nor the strength for repairs. Across the road were nearly 45,000 Filipino prisoners in worse shape than we were. The lines of their burial detail were much longer than ours. The Japanese were treating them even more callously. Of the perhaps 9,000 Americans, we were among the most healthy of mind as well as body, mainly because of Colonel Miller's organization and care in Bataan and Camp O'Donnell.

Sometime at the end of the second week, the Japanese sent each barracks leader a sheet of paper with a list of occupations. I could find nothing appropriate to check. But at college I had minored in education, so I checked "teacher," sensei. I was not aware that teacher, soldier, and magistrate ranked as the three most honored professions in Japan. When asked what I taught, I replied, "Singing." Some of the prisoners laughed. Little did I know that the phrase "sensei, teacher of singing" would somewhat smooth my life as a prisoner in the months ahead.

On May 5 a list came from Japanese headquarters requiring 300 men to leave O'Donnell on a detail to build bridges. Along with the carpenters, the mechanics, and the other skilled men went one sensei. All but 25 men were from the 2 tank battalions. By the nature of their work, tankers were the best suited to the detail and were in better shape. Ken Porwoll, a sergeant in the 194th, crawled out of St. Peter's Ward to go on the detail—anything to get out of O'Donnell. Two days later a line of Ford trucks took us out down the dirt road. We were all so exhausted with hunger and illness that we hardly noticed the countryside, green with the onset of the rainy season. In Manila we were fed well and herded for the night into a large, ramshackle building that had been a shoe factory.

On our way south the next day we were driven down the Escolta, Manila's main avenue. The Filipinos threw us fruit and rice cakes and gave the V sign. When we paused at an intersection, a Filipino barber shaving a Japanese officer—one could tell by his boots—held open a pair of scissors as a V sign. At one food stand the tossing of food became too open, and the guards bailed off the trucks, smashed the stand, and shouted at the Filipinos, who were ducking out of sight.

25

BUILDING BRIDGES

W E FELT HOPEFUL as the guards dropped us off in the main street of Calauan, a town 40 miles southeast of Manila, and turned us over to the Japanese combat engineers. We were tired from the long truck ride, and some men had to be held up. The Japanese engineers could not understand why we were in such bad shape, starved and sick from three months of half rations or less on Bataan, before the Hike and the month in O'Donnell. Many of us bled from sores around the mouth. We had scurvy, pellagra, dysentery, malaria, and beriberi. Nevertheless, we felt hopeful there on the main street of Calauan. The quiet, prosperous town was clean. The air was sweet with the smell of fruit trees and of the cooking fires of coconut husks.

The commander of the Japanese engineers, Captain Wakamori, spoke to us briefly in Japanese, translated into stilted English by the interpreter. It was a welcome, not like the harsh denunciation screamed at us when we entered O'Donnell. For the rest of our time under his command, Captain Wakamori spoke careful idiomatic English. After his welcome, he motioned us through a fence and into the cabildo, the town hall. The curious Filipino townspeople smiled to us reassuringly before they dispersed.

In the cabildo some of us slept on the ground floor of cement, others on the wooden floor of the second story. Filipino workmen brought in bundles of woven split-bamboo mats for us, and a detail of the engineers brought in armloads of old, gray army blankets, captured U.S. issue. The building was clean and spacious. When it rained, the corrugated iron roof drummed, but it was solid and watertight. The thick, greenish white adobe walls kept us fairly cool even in the hottest weather, and there were enough windows to let the evening breeze flow through the building. Down the main street toward the east we could see the bleached adobe walls of the fortress-church and its adjoining

Dr. Mariano Marfori (left) and Dr. Ricardo de Guzman, April 1967, in front of the war memorial to the citizens of Calauan, who were killed during a battle between Japanese and American forces, February 1945.

convent and rectory. Rising in pure curves behind the church was the volcanic peak of Mount Banahao, haloed by fine, light clouds. West over a schoolhouse, Mount Maquiling stood against the sky.

Filipino workmen brought in two large cast-iron pots and helped our cooks set up a kitchen. We received regular rations three times a day. The first few days we got ordinary cooked rice, enough to keep

Dr. Ricardo de Guzman, in Calauan, 1991. Photo courtesy of Dr. Ricardo de Guzman.

our shrunken stomachs quiet, and thick vegetable soup, usually squash. Later Dr. Mariano Marfori, with Captain Wakamori, insisted that we received palay, the unhusked rice, and limes to cure our bleeding gums. The pellagra and scurvy slowly receded, although the palay was hard on those of us with dysentery.

When Dr. Marfori and Dr. Ricardo de Guzman discovered our

condition, they brought their nurse, Maria Ravelo. In her starched white uniform and pinned cap, she seemed like someone out of a dream. Dr. Marfori, padrone of the town and godfather to many of the young people of Calauan, seemed to have more medicine than we saw for the rest of the war. Two war prisoners died early in our stay at Calauan. They were buried by the local priest, Father Nazario Atienza. Captain Wakamori and some of his men came to the burial.

Despite the rule that we were not to receive anything from the Filipinos nor to talk to them, the townspeople of Calauan found ways to get food and medicine to us, and they smiled and waved as they passed along main street. Under Captain Wakamori, the Japanese engineers gradually ignored these rules. At the bridge-building site one mile north, the guards quietly allowed the Filipinos to bring us extra food. To save face for the guards, the Filipinos devised several tricks. For instance, during a break a calesa would drive up to cross the river on the rickety old plank bridge next to the bridge we were building. Pineapples might be piled high in the back of the calesa, and the driver would whip his little horse, and a few pineapples would fall off as the calesa bounced across on the rough planks. Corporal Ishitani would grin and call out, "Grabbo sabisu" ("Grab gifts"), and we would share several fat pineapples that would have brought good prices at the markets in the nearby villages.

In the first couple of weeks we badly needed extra food. The work was exhausting, especially carrying the bridge timber into position. Often when we went to the pile of timbers that the trucks had brought down from Paete, we found that the Filipinos had slipped by, leaving mangoes, bananas, and cigarettes between the timbers, sometimes with a note of encouragement from the local guerrilla leader, El Cobra. Eventually, when the Filipino townspeople were sure that Captain Wakamori and his men would not take it amiss, two or three girls would arrive in a calesa at each break period. They would pass out pieces of fried bananas coated with raw sugar or rice cakes sweetened with coconut milk. Of course, they observed the proper formalities. First they offered food to the engineers, who would gravely accept their share. Then Corporal Ishitani would wave his hand toward us: "Sabisu, America." He would smile broadly and say, "Yoi, yoi!" ("Very good, very good!"), as though he had arranged the whole thing.

We wanted to come to work for the extra food during the breaks, and the Japanese officer would allow the senior American officer to decide who was strong enough to work. When dysentery acted up, the guards would merely point off into the jungle. They did not yell at us to hurry, nor did they check on us. Escape would have been easy. For most of us this period of four and one-half months was the only time we were in close contact with an elite corps of the Japanese army. These Japanese officers and soldiers under Captain Wakamori had remained capable of both independent action and sensitive feelings toward others.

Captain Wakamori and Lieutenant Miyosato were perhaps five feet eight or nine, lithe and muscular in build. They were graduates of the Imperial University of Tokyo, the Japanese equivalent of Oxford or Cambridge. They spoke English well. Wakamori's hair was close-cropped, rather than shaved in the style of the fanatical Japanese officers. He smiled easily. He was immaculate, often wearing white knit gloves, a white shirt open at the neck, and drill shorts in the British style. He never referred to us as horyo. He never wore side arms or a sword when he came to visit or inspect us, unless he was officially dressed, as during a visit by Colonel Kamia.

On one of the first days working on the bridge, Sergeant Bob Stewart from Janesville, Wisconsin, and I were driving pilings with a heavy wooden cap driver. We raised it by hand and slammed it down on the piling. It was very hard work. When I was trimming the top of a piling with a stubborn Japanese saw, a Japanese engineer was trying to tell us what to do, but we couldn't understand him. The interpreter, Suzuki, gave us a confusing translation. I muttered to Bob, "I wish the bastards would use English."

Immediately a clear voice said in excellent English, "It would be much better, wouldn't it?" It was the courteous Lieutenant Miyosato, with no rancor in his voice. If I had said such a thing in the presence of the Japanese officers of O'Donnell or later at Cabanatuan, I would have been instantly and thoroughly beaten, perhaps executed.

Later Manila ordered a guard at all times because guerrillas could easily have approached through the thick forest to within 20 feet of the bridge detail. The Japanese were offering 5,000 pesos for the guerrilla leader El Cobra. Even the Japanese engineers thought it ridiculous when Three-Star Private Nikki arrived with a rifle to guard us at the bridge site. Nikki was much amused by Sergeant Larry Jordan from Chicago, who explained to him that MacArthur had left Corregidor to get whiskey, without which Americans couldn't shoot straight.

Larry kidded Nikki about the Buddhist amulet on a thong around Nikki's neck. Nikki looked at Larry for a long moment and pointed to the medal of the Virgin Mary that hung on Larry's neck along with his dog tags.

"Nanni?" ("What?")

"It is to turn the bullet aside," Larry said.

"Soka?" ("Is that so?") Nikki held his amulet toward Larry. "Onaji." ("The same.") The amulet was dented.

Only one guard walked patrol around the cabildo at night. Sometimes in the evening a group of us sat outside the cabildo. One or two of the other prisoners would ask me to sing, and gradually the whole group joined in. Across the stream by the mayor's house Filipino girls would gather to listen and, when the guard had passed by, to throw food across the stream and over the fence to us. The guard seemed to enjoy the singing too, and he never stopped us. The Japanese engineers were sometimes low on food also, and we shared ours with them.

Occasionally, in the early evening Captain Wakamori would pay a courtesy visit to the senior officer of the American contingent, Lieutenant Colonel Theodore Wickord. He would suggest that some of his American friends join him in a walk outside of town. Then those of us who had the energy would join him. The bright tropical moon, cool evening air, and the fresh smell of growing things were a delight. The captain would ask us to sit by the roadside. He would pass around some cigarettes and ask us to sing. He was familiar with many of our songs and especially enjoyed folk songs, spirituals, and the songs of Stephen Foster. Then we would stroll back to the cabildo to sleep, with the one guard making his token rounds.

Work on the bridge was sometimes interrupted by the heavy rains of the monsoon season. Then the Japanese officer would motion us to take our tools and find shelter under trees. During one downpour First Sergeant Teramura motioned me into the toolshed with him, and we sat on the dry, sandy floor together. We both knew that the bridge-building detail would end in two or three months and I would be shipped back to one of the prison camps. Speaking slowly, he said, "Learn language and do as told. Then you get along well." He put a cigarette into a long holder and grinned with it in his mouth at a jaunty angle, like Franklin Roosevelt. Then, more earnestly, he repeated his advice. He talked with me about a naval battle. Smoothing out the sand, he sketched a map and pointed out where Midway was. Whoever

won that battle, he thought, would win the war. He said he was tired
of war.

Perhaps a week later during a break Lieutenant Miyosato sat on
one of the bridge timbers next to me. He held out his fist. "Before the
war, Japan was like my fist, clenched so. But now. . . ." He held his
hand open with the fingers spread. His other hand chopped at each
finger one by one. "This," he said, "is Japan today. We should not be
at war." Japan had been defeated at Midway on June 6, 1942.

26

THE TWO FIESTAS OF SAN ISIDRO

*T*OWARD THE END of May 1942 Mayor Marfori, who was not related to Dr. Marfori, invited Captain Wakamori and his men to a fiesta celebrating the patron saint of Calauan, San Isidro, the guardian saint of agriculture. Captain Wakamori accepted, without breaking any rules, because he was authorized to declare rest days. He asked the mayor if he could bring his American friends. It was a stratagem, understood by both parties, to provide us with a feast.

Before daybreak on the morning of the fiesta the Filipinos began to gather in the school yard directly across the street from us. The women carried baskets of fruit on their heads, and the men began to roast young pigs on spits over slow, open fires. Those savory odors drifting from the school yard became almost unbearable. We pressed against the fence to look at the roasting pigs and the piles of bananas, avocados, papayas, mangoes, and pineapples. The Japanese sentry smiled and said, "Mati, mati." ("Wait, wait.")

Captain Wakamori came to the opening in the fence a little before 9 A.M. Would some of us like to accompany him to the fiesta mass to be offered by Padre Atienza? Many of us walked with him to the old Spanish church, as the bell in the tower pealed. Along both sides of the street young Filipino men smiled and waved, though they were forbidden to talk to us. Old women in black, with mantillas over their heads, and well-to-do young ladies, wearing the Balintawak mestiza dress with the butterfly sleeves and long skirt, smiled shyly at us. Dr. de Guzman, Dr. Marfori, and Mayor Marfori, in crisp barong Tagalog shirts with cuff links and dark pants, bowed to us.

After mass we walked back to the school yard and sat cross-legged on the grass talking with the Japanese engineers. We avoided talking with the Filipinos, as they moved among us serving a light noon meal of fried rice with bits of pork and papayas and avocados. Coffee heavily

131

Dr. Mariano Marfori in his yard, circa 1967, in Calauan. In the background is the repaired Catholic church bombed in February 1945. Photo courtesy of Carmen Marfori Madrigal.

sugared was poured into our canteen cups, and they passed out cigarillos. So we rested in the shade and talked until the heat of the day began to wane. The Japanese soldiers and some of the more healthy Americans played softball. Captain Wakamori played one inning with each team. He pitched for the American team, and one of his fast throws hit the batter, one of his own men. He walked directly to the man and bowed in apology, before the Filipino umpire sent him to first base. At the end of seven innings the mayor called the game to a halt. I can't remember who won. We cheered both sides.

The main meal of the fiesta was ready. Filipinos, Americans, and Japanese sat on the grass, and young Filipino men in white smocks brought us food, all we could eat—roast suckling pig, fried chicken, fried rice, fried bananas with raw sugar, and the fresh fruits. We continued to eat, even when our good sense warned us to stop. I knew that my dysentery would give me a violent reaction the next day.

In June a well-organized guerrilla band broke into the bridge-building work camp at Lumban, a few miles east of Calauan. This work camp was composed of 150 men from the original work detail of 300 prisoners from Camp O'Donnell. In the attack several Japanese guards were killed, and some were wounded. The guerrillas intended to free all the prisoners at Lumban, but they had not understood how weak these men were after the fighting in Bataan and the Hike. Most of them were in no condition to attempt escape, and the men who were relatively strong refused to leave, because they were aware that whoever was left behind would probably be tortured and executed. The guerrillas were not equipped to carry so many weakened prisoners, and eventually they gave up their plan and left. But one man went with them. Early that morning the Japanese guards discovered his escape.

Ten war prisoners were selected at random and sentenced to be executed the following day. Colonel Kamia, who was in charge of all war prisoners building bridges in the Philippines, arrived from Manila to supervise the execution. The ten victims were forced to dig their own graves. The rest of the men in the bridge-building detail were ordered to stand at attention and watch while a machine gun cut down the ten prisoners standing at their graves. Among those forced to watch was Eddie Betts, who became a friend of mine later at Cabanatuan Prison Camp and at the Fukuoka Prison Camp in Japan. His brother was one of the ten victims.

On the day after that execution, work was interrupted at our camp at Calauan. Colonel Kamia selected representatives from three groups: Captain Wakamori, as the commander of the company of Japanese engineers; Lieutenant Colonel Wickord, as the top-ranking American officer; and Dr. Marfori, as a Filipino resident of Calauan. Colonel Kamia showed them the graves, explained what had been done, and ordered them to report this reprisal to their groups.

Soon afterward an incident at Calauan revealed Captain Wakamori's mettle. In the June heat we were resting during the two-hour noon period. A thin prisoner suddenly made a run for it. We had been worried about him because he had the glazed, faraway look in his eyes that showed he was dangerously low, that his will to live was decaying. He was probably out of his mind from cerebral malaria and malnutrition. He had no chance of escaping, but he climbed over the low wire fence of the cabildo and began to run past the market toward the church. The sole Japanese guard called for him to stop. Then he unslung his rifle and placed it on the ground and enfolded the running, stumbling American in his arms.

The actions of this sick man had to be taken seriously. It was an attempt to escape, and by Colonel Kamia's rule, both the prisoner and the nine others in his "blood brother group" should be executed. The plaza came to life. Out of his house across the square came Captain Wakamori, without his Nambu automatic or his sword. Sergeant Teramura appeared. Dr. Marfori came running from his house nearby. After a brief command to the guard, Captain Wakamori took the prisoner by the left arm, and Dr. Marfori took his right arm. Colonel Wickord came up with a guard from the gate of the cabildo fence. The captain and Dr. Marfori supported the fevered and sagging prisoner, as the whole group moved slowly through the gate into the cabildo. The prisoner was put in a small room.

We prisoners stood around in a half trance and discussed the incident, carefully not mentioning the reprisal we were sure would follow. Bridge building was forgotten for that day. I and some others went back to sitting under the shade of an acacia tree beside the cabildo. I belonged to the blood brother group of the man who had tried to escape.

In a little while Captain Wakamori's 1940 black Ford sedan drove into the square and parked in front of the captain's house. The Japanese driver opened the rear door and bowed as Captain Wakamori, in full uniform with sword and holstered Nambu, came out of the house. He waited until Dr. Marfori, in a formal white barong Tagalog tunic and dark trousers, joined him. Without a word they entered the car and drove north toward Manila. The interpreter, Suzuki, watched all this without expression and then climbed on his bicycle and went off, presumably to write a report to Colonel Kamia.

Late that evening the black Ford returned to the plaza and let out the captain and Dr. Marfori. We were ordered to a tenko, a formation at which we counted off. Colonel Wickord announced in his flowery rhetorical way that, through the intercession of Dr. Marfori and Captain Wakamori at General Homma's headquarters in Manila, there would be no reprisals against anyone, neither the fevered man in the cell nor any of us. I stood in the soft night air and breathed in thankfulness and smelled the faint odors of the rice paddies and the fruit trees.

Later we learned by the rumors of the "bamboo telegraph" that Dr. Marfori had claimed that the prisoner was insane. The Japanese command decided that an American might well be insane. Therefore, no action was to be taken. A day or so later when the regular weekly truck went north, the sick prisoner was sent to the Cabanatuan Prison Camp, where he soon died.

Meanwhile, the rice paddies were coming into full head. Even the dikes were green with the constant rain. Each harvest day was a minor festival in itself. Young men would take turns playing a guitar and singing harvest songs with everyone, while they threshed and sacked the rice. Then each woman would put a shallow basket on her head, fitting snugly by a supporting band. Two older children would help her raise a heavy sack of rice into the basket. In a quick step, almost a trot, the woman would carry off the rice. These women passed us on the road, smiling serenely at us even under their heavy load.

In most of the paddies the Filipinos raised fish along with the two crops of rice. When the harvest was done, the small irrigation locks were raised and the water receded. The younger children gathered the fish and took them to be dried. When the rice and fish had been harvested, the carabao were turned out into the paddies to graze. Their manure fertilized the paddies for the next planting. After the paddies had been plowed by the same patient carabao, the whole community joined in planting the new crop. Again the young men played guitars and sang while everyone quickly and rhythmically set down the new shoots of rice. Then the irrigation ditches were opened, and the paddies gently flooded.

When the townspeople of Calauan heard that we would be moving to Batangas, Mayor Marfori paid another call on Captain Wakamori. San Isidro, it seemed, had more than one fiesta at Calauan. Mayor Marfori regretted that he hadn't called it to the attention of the captain sooner, but the fiesta would take place the very next day. Again Captain Wakamori accepted the invitation and asked if he could bring his American friends.

That second fiesta was as delightful as the first. We again trooped down the main street to mass and then returned to the school yard to rest in the shade and watch the spits turning over the fires. When the feasting started, one of the young Filipino men seemed strangely familiar to me. I became conscious that he had noticed me. I had put away almost as much food as I could hold, and then he leaned over my shoulder and placed another helping of roast suckling pig and fried rice in my mess kit. In a soft voice he said, "Old friend, sing 'Old Kentucky Home,' no?" and walked nonchalantly away with a broad smile on his face.

Suddenly, my memory clicked. Back on Bataan I had become friends with an alert young sergeant in a Philippine army engineer unit. When we had a fairly quiet stretch of time behind the Pilar-Bagac line, we used to gather in an open space in the jungle and tell stories and occasionally sing the campfire favorites. The Filipino soldiers and non-coms from the nearby engineer unit came first to listen and later to join in. Sergeant Mateo Ladre never failed to ask me to sing "Old Kentucky Home." He had told me that he was from Calauan. Now I realized that this smiling young man in the white smock was Sergeant Mateo Ladre. It was dangerous for him to be at the fiesta. He came by again to put some cigarillos in my lap.

Out of the corner of my mouth I muttered, "Mateo, we are being watched."

"Ah, old friend, we must trust San Isidro," he said lightly.

A few minutes later Captain Wakamori got to his feet and suggested that we sing together. He turned to me and asked me to sing "Old Kentucky Home." For a moment I felt as though he was reading my mind. Then I stood up, as a trio of Filipinos with guitars joined me, and I started to sing. The dusk was coming rapidly, and out of the corner of my eye I saw Mateo grinning. Before I finished the song, he had drifted into the trees at the far edge of the school yard and was gone.

The Japanese engineers sang their songs for us: "Umabi no ute" ("The Song of the Sea Beach") and a folk song, "Watashi wa ju roku," about a soldier asking a girl if he could call on her father to seek her hand, to which she replies that she is only 16 and her father might not approve. We all applauded loudly. Then two Filipinos came forward with guitars, and a group of young Filipino men and women danced for us. The dances were a curious blend of Moorish and Filipino, spirited and yet with a touch of formality. The engineers and war prisoners applauded for a long time.

Captain Wakamori announced that we should sing together. And Japanese and Filipino and American sang old-time American songs. In accordance with my designation as a music teacher, I led the group and chose the songs, in wonder at the harmony of our three different groups in the midst of war.

27

CALAUAN REVISITED

AFTER THE WAR, in October 1945, I returned to Calauan with three friends, fresh from the miseries of prison compounds in the Philippines and in Japan: Bill McKeon from Crystal, Minnesota; Joe Errington from Salinas, California; and one of the few survivors of the massacre on Palawan, Dick Walker, the prewar tennis star, also from Salinas. We decided to escape the dreariness of the repatriation area at Muntinlupa. Dick Walker had been listed as dead, and until the monster of army red tape recognized that he was alive, he couldn't get transportation back to the United States.

Full of high spirits, we set off from Muntinlupa, hitching a ride on one of the many army DUKS, large trucks with a boat body and a propeller in addition to the usual wheels. We piled in, with Filipino families, chickens, and boxes, and set out along the dusty old military highway. The macadam was pretty well repaired in places. The weather was beautiful, and we could see Laguna de Bay, the huge lake east of us, and rice paddies and villages and occasional coconut groves. Army trucks passed us with a wave, and once in a while columns of carabao carts held us up until we could pass. I think the DUK turned off near Los Banos, and then we shared the hire of a calesa.

A mile north of Calauan, we found the bridge we had built with the Japanese engineers. It was still able to bear heavy truck traffic. When we turned the last bend in the road, we saw that the cabildo, where we had been quartered, was rubble. The schoolhouse was ashes. The mango trees and papayas and limes had been partly blown down by artillery shells. Some were split as though by lightning. An Army Signal Corps outfit was encamped in tents on the now shabby lawn. We looked sadly at the school yard where we had feasted in honor of the gentle patron saint of agriculture, San Isidro.

At the far end of the plaza, the church, the convent, and the rectory

137

Catholic church in Calauan under repair after being bombed as the result of a battle between Japanese and American forces in February 1945. Photo courtesy of Carmen Marfori Madrigal.

still stood, though the church had been badly damaged. Only charred and ash-strewn earth marked the house that Captain Wakamori had occupied. The smell of the smashed, burnt town clung to everything. Our clothes kept it even after we left. Lean-tos and shelters of blackened corrugated metal roofing, perhaps taken from the ruins of the cabildo, had sprung up around the plaza.

We waited outside the hovels, where a young Filipino boy asked us to be patient for a minute, and then Maria Ravelo, the nurse working for Dr. Marfori and Dr. de Guzman, came out of a hovel, shining and clean in a dress made of flour sacking. The faded Pillsbury label was visible on the back. She said, "Oh, Bernardo, they are all gone." Six or seven months earlier her whole family had been executed with others in front of the church.

We went together to find Dr. Marfori. He still had his hacienda a mile west of town, from which Yamashita and MacArthur had successively commanded their armies. But his handsome house on the plaza was gutted. He led us behind the ruined house and dug up from its hiding place a container of strong rice wine. He told us about the help from the signal corps outfit and introduced us to the captain and some of his men. They had been transferred all the way from Europe. The captain invited us to dinner.

We walked about the plaza and went to Dr. Juan Schultz's house, which rose above the remains of the burnt shops and houses. Dr. Schultz was a wealthy German-Filipino landowner who had often visited us on rest days, always bringing a box of cigars. Now he was sitting in his one remaining handsome chair at a large mahogany table. He had paper and pen on the table, but he stared blankly into space. The tall, silver-haired old man looked dignified and commanding, but that day he was empty, and we did not linger there.

After dinner the four of us hitched a ride back toward Muntinlupa. We didn't reach Muntinlupa because we found an army outfit having a party. Quite quickly, having no tolerance for alcohol then, Bill and I found something important to quarrel about, went outside, and fell on our faces and slept.

28

THE FAIR ONE

*T*HE DAY BEFORE WE LEFT for the port city of Batangas, Captain Wakamori and Lieutenant Colonel Wickord drove ahead of us to find quarters for the engineers and the prisoners. On July 1, 1942, Sergeant Teramura sorted us out in front of the cabildo and ordered us into the trucks. The engineers loaded their equipment and climbed into the trucks. Most of the townspeople waved and called farewell. We waved, sad to be leaving. The line of trucks moved out onto the dusty highway, and about two and a half hours later we were pulling into the outskirts of Batangas, 30 miles southwest of Calauan.

We drew up in front of a large, modern school building shaded by acacias, mangoes, and papayas. The Japanese took over the first floor, and we moved into classrooms and offices on the second floor. The building was solid enough to be cool, and the rooms were clean and comfortable. From the second floor we could look out across the lower part of the town to the harbor and the sea beyond the headlands. This small city, the capital of the province of Batangas, had about 13,000 people before the invasion. The Japanese navy had shelled the town, and the artillery of the landing force had destroyed more buildings. Many Filipinos had left and were now returning to the city. When the weather was good, we often slept outside on the trim grass lawns, and the engineers made no objection. We soon found that the word had gone ahead of us to the people of Batangas. Our Filipino friends at Calauan made sure that we would be looked after on this new job. At Batangas we were split into two working parties, repairing a bridge between Batangas and Lipa and several bridges to the west of Batangas on the road along the shore to Lemery.

We came to know several of the younger soldiers of the combat engineers. For these privates the problems of rank were irksome, but Private Son and Private Misakawa were cheerful. They tried out their

English on us and were friendly around the edges of army discipline. Private Son and First Sergeant Saccone of Company C, 194th Tank Battalion, now our acting mess sergeant, became long-term friends. Son had been a cook in the Japanese merchant marine before the war and knew several ports in the United States. As chief cook for the engineers, he had considerable authority, despite his rank as private. Son used to sneak some extra stew into Sergeant Saccone's mess kit and laugh and laugh, as if he had put something over on the army system.

Private Misakawa, who spoke good English, had been well along in a university in Japan when he was drafted. He and I talked often about what we had done before the war. One night I had just fallen asleep on my blanket outside the school buildings when I felt someone gently shaking me. I looked up, and Misakawa said, "Very quiet." He turned on a shaded flashlight and looked warily around. Then he reached into his knapsack and pulled out a baseball. Almost reverently he put it in my hand and shone the dim light on it. I saw the autographs of Babe Ruth, Lefty Gomez, Charlie Gerhinger, Lou Gehrig, and others. Misakawa told me that he had served as a batboy for the American League All Star Team touring Japan in 1934. He had carried his autographed baseball with him at all times, even in combat. He was especially proud that he had met Babe Ruth.

Captain Wakamori gave us the Fourth of July as a rest day. We needed it. Apparently, the change of water had given many of us dysentery again. I lay on the lawn under a tree, exhausted from bowel cramps and wishing I had the appetite and strength to eat and keep down some rice. Wild Bill Boyd, nearly as sick, told me he couldn't eat two cooked eggs he had acquired. We made a solemn trade—his gold for my silver—ate, and felt better. Private Son, sitting on a second-story windowsill began to play his harmonica. Bill and I grinned at each other when he played "Red River Valley" and "Pretty Redwing." Bill said, "Does it make you homesick for Minnesota?" It was a very quiet Fourth of July for us.

Almost as soon as we reached Batangas, a group of nuns paid a call on Captain Wakamori. They brought gifts to the commander, knowing the trickling-down custom whereby engineers and prisoners received some of the extra things. As the days passed, the nuns often invited Captain Wakamori to their convent for tea. He was accompanied by an American officer. Soon the nuns began to supply us with medicine,

coffee, sugar, salt, and mended clothes that they had scoured the countryside to find for us. We were down to rags by that time. Bridge
building in the tropics had just about finished the tattered uniforms we
had been wearing on the way out of Bataan.

The Japanese allowed the nuns much freedom, especially the nuns
who were citizens of nations not at war with Japan. On the first day
the food and clothing were brought by a nun from Ireland and some
convent-school girls in white blouses and blue skirts. They were accompanied by a very fair and lovely young woman who seemed quite
different from the dark-haired, quick-smiling Filipino girls. Her name
was Lou Ashley. We looked forward to seeing the Fair One, as some
of the men called her.

The large Convent of the Good Shepherd stood near the northern
edge of the city. The convent school was especially for girls who were
orphans or who had been abandoned by their parents. The buildings,
with faded orange tile roofs, were very old and the Spanish-Moorish
architecture was exotic against the rest of Batangas. A stone wall green
with moss enclosed both school and convent, and ornate ironwork
rose from the top of the wall. Because the Good Shepherd nuns were
then under the jurisdiction of the St. Paul, Minnesota, province, I was
especially pleased when Captain Wakamori gave permission on our
last day in Batangas for us to attend mass at the convent.

About 50 of us went to a very early Sunday mass. A guard walked
with us, and the nuns were careful to ask his permission for anything
that concerned us. When we had filed through the massive gates and
were waiting to enter the chapel, the guard came to me and said, "The
Dai Ichi wishes to speak to you." He took me to the mother superior,
who asked me to help with serving mass. It was a strange congregation—the schoolgirls, the war prisoners of many different faiths, the
nuns, and one Japanese guard. A Belgian priest offered the mass, and
he seemed pleased to have someone act as a server. During the mass
the nuns sang several hymns well, especially "Salve Regina," one of the
earliest and most beautiful of hymns in its Gregorian simplicity and
clarity.

After the mass, as we were leaving the chapel, one of the nuns
stepped forward from a table loosely covered with a large, white cloth.
She dipped her body in a slight, old-fashioned curtsy to our Japanese
guard and offered him some sugar cakes and a hard-boiled egg. He
bowed to her and looked over her shoulder at the shrouded table.

"Would you give some to our American friends?" he asked politely. The nun beamed, gave him the egg and the sugar cakes, and turned to the table. With the help of the Fair One, Lou Ashley, she gently whisked aside the cloth to disclose many of the small cakes arranged in a pyramid at one end of the table, a large pan filled with hard-boiled eggs, and two huge cut-glass bowls filled with pieces of mango and pineapple, each with a little bamboo skewer. We crowded around like restrained vultures. As we filed back to the school buildings through the awakening town in the fresh, cool air of the predawn sky, Jeremiah Collins, the Irish professional soldier from the 31st Infantry who had befriended me on the way out of Bataan, was still nibbling on a sugar cake. He turned to us and announced, "Sure and the singing of the nuns was equal to the singing of the angels at Bethlehem."

Under the watchful eye of Sergeant Teramura, we collected our few belongings and climbed into the waiting trucks. The sun was barely up when we pulled out of Batangas and headed north and then east to Candelaria.

In the autumn of 1945, when I was returning to America on the hospital repatriation ship, the *Klipfontein*, I met Sister St. Vitalis, one of the nuns from the Convent of the Good Shepherd in Batangas. She told me the story of the Fair One.

In Asia before the Second World War, unwanted newborn children, particularly baby girls, were sometimes abandoned. According to Sister St. Vitalis, an old sergeant of the 31st Regiment was meandering back to the Spanish barracks in Manila after a heavy night. He came across one of the bridges spanning the Pasig River, which separated the old walled city from the newer part. A young woman on the bridge was holding a baby in her arms and looking down at the dark surface of the river, still shadowed in the pale light before the dawn. The old sergeant of the "Thirsty-First" tipped his hat to her and stopped. The woman held out the baby: "You buy?" The sergeant stood almost at attention for a moment and then fumbled in his pocket. He held out a 50 centavos piece, about 25 cents in U.S. currency. The woman thrust the child into his arms and walked away. The old sergeant carried the baby back to his barracks.

The sergeant's company raised the baby. The 31st Infantry Regiment, the Foreign Legion of the U.S. Army, had never served on U.S. soil. Many of the soldiers in the 31st had never been in the United States—White Russians, Irish, German, English, Italian, and even men without nationality. No one asked questions about the background of a man in this regiment. They named the child Lou Ellen, and for five or six years they protected her and lavished her with affection. Then the company commander told Sergeant Ashley that it was time for Lou to be placed elsewhere to be educated. A group of soldiers went with Sergeant Ashley to call on the mother superior of the Convent of the Good Shepherd in Manila. She told them she would gladly accept the child without charge, but the men of the 31st raffled a car and presented the proceeds to the mother superior.

When Sergeant Ashley escorted Lou to the convent, the nuns asked her, "What is your name?" She answered proudly, "My name is Lou Ashley." She tugged at the sergeant's sleeve: "This is my dad." Every Sunday while Lou was growing up, Lou's "dad" came to see her. Lou was entering her collegiate training as a nurse in 1938 when Sergeant Ashley died. Upon graduation she was sent to Batangas to work and teach under the jurisdiction of the convent there, where we met her in the summer of 1942.

In early 1945 when the Japanese navy made its suicidal stand in Manila, the Fair One was there caring for the wounded American soldiers. During one heavy artillery duel, many were killed. One of them was Lou Ashley.

29

BUILDING MORE BRIDGES

CANDELARIA TURNED OUT to be smaller and less prosperous than Calauan or Batangas. Perhaps because it was on the main highway between Manila and Legaspi, at the southeastern end of Luzon, it was watched more closely by the Japanese occupation. The Filipino townspeople kept to themselves. We were quartered apart from the town in a dilapidated old copra warehouse, rather like an immensely long barn with no hayloft and few windows. The heavy, sweet smell of dried coconut hung in the air. At night we were shut in, and the warehouse grew hot and stuffy.

For a while food was scarce for us and the Japanese engineers. Captain Wakamori came to the warehouse one evening and made a brief apology to us. He came down with an ear infection and for a week was unable to get medicine from headquarters in Manila. Malaria had flared up among the prisoners, and many of us came down with dysentery again. The Japanese medic with the engineers could only offer us his own homemade charcoal as a medicine. The engineers who were sick were even more troubled than we were: soldiers of the Imperial Army were not supposed to get sick. We were at least allowed illness.

Many of us began to show signs of pellagra and scurvy. I had a recurrence of malaria and dysentery, and sores appeared inside my mouth, on my lips, and even in my throat. I had always felt a little impatient toward men who seemed to give up. But after Candelaria I was never again scornful of another man for his lack of will to fight to live. In *Barbed-Wire Surgeon* Dr. Alfred A. Weinstein speaks of his initial scorn for the prisoners who could not control their bowels, until he too was stricken with dysentery. I could not keep down the rice. I remember lying in the copra warehouse and thinking that nothing mattered anymore, when Sergeant Rick Errington, Joe Errington's brother, came

145

and squatted next to me. He didn't say much. He began to spoon lukewarm bean broth into my mouth. I don't remember how many times he persisted until I regained enough strength to try rice.

Then help arrived from Calauan. We were astonished and delighted to see Dr. Marfori walk into the warehouse one morning with Captain Wakamori, pale but on his feet once more, and Lieutenant Miyosato, who had been spending most of his time keeping track of the lumber mill up north at Paete, on the eastern shore of Laguna de Bay. Dr. Marfori had medicine and kindness and confidence for all of us. He looked at the sores in the mouths of those of us who had not gone to work that day and spoke one word to the captain: "Limes."

The next day a potato sack of limes arrived with instructions for Sergeant Saccone. Dr. Marfori insisted that we eat a whole lime three times a day, rind and all. When I sucked the first piece of lime, I screamed with pain. It was like pouring iodine on the open sores on my lips, in my mouth, and in my throat. But despite the pain, we all persisted. Gradually we could go to work and help with the lightest chores. Until Dr. Marfori suggested it, we hadn't thought of eating the dried coconut stacked at one end of the warehouse. Soaked and then chewed slowly, it was bland and sweet and filling.

Once when a sick man was not moving fast enough, one of the Japanese privates batted the prisoner on the head. Sergeant Teramura just took his long cigarette holder out of his mouth and looked at the private. Not a word was said. The private slunk off. Not one of the engineers ever touched us except for this occasion.

There was a fiesta in honor of the town's patron saint. But the presence of Colonel Kamia, down from Manila on an inspection tour, gave an edge of military restraint to the joyousness usual at a Filipino fiesta. A baseball game was interrupted by Colonel Kamia's arrival. Everything came to a halt while the fawning interpreter Suzuki rushed up to bring him a chair. The game resumed, but suddenly Kamia gestured and said a word to one of his staff, and all the American war prisoners were ordered off the field. Horyo were unworthy to compete with the Japanese imperial soldiers. Filipinos, prisoners, and engineers stood frozen for a moment, and then the few American prisoners who had felt strong enough to play walked off the field. The game went on for one more inning. Then Captain Wakamori, stiff and embarrassed, announced that it was time to eat. Kamia sat in his chair and glowered at us, occasionally raising a hand to feel his waxed mustache or adjust his visored cap on his freshly shaven head. Suzuki served his food, taking it officiously from the Filipino servers. Kamia ate sparingly, thrust the plate at Suzuki, rose abruptly, and stalked off without a glance at his staff, who scurried after him. In a few minutes we all relaxed and got back to eating the roast pig and chicken and fruit.

For a few days I went to work, even though I was still shaky on my feet. Sergeant Teramura assigned me the small task of building the fire to boil water for our break and then brewing the tea or coffee. Dr. Marfori had apparently talked with both the mayor of Candelaria and with Captain Wakamori, for at our breaks Filipino girls brought rice cakes, fried sugared bananas, coffee, and raw sugar. We had all become used to drinking coffee loaded with raw sugar, the way the Japanese engineers liked it. From the middle of August our health got better.

Every morning the work detail climbed into the trucks and went out of town several miles to a large concrete bridge that needed extensive repair. The work was different from what we had been doing on the timber trestle bridges at Calauan and Batangas. At Candelaria we made concrete in a very large wooden box like a flat-bottomed, square-ended boat. The concrete was mixed by hand. Wheelbarrows brought sand and cement, men threw in buckets of water, and then the toughest work of all began: mixing the mortar by hand. The engineers fed extra rations to the men who did this work. Bob Schultz, from the 192nd Tank Battalion, was especially good at wielding the short Japanese shovel and rhythmically turning the mortar.

> One, two—
> Rice and stew.
> Three, four—
> Give us more.
> Five, six—
> It makes us sick.

The engineers grinned in sympathy with Bob and the other mixers as they chanted this little rhyme. When the bridge was again sound and the surface had set, we removed the crude shuttering from the hardened concrete and cleaned up. Then we began work on a timber bridge on the outskirts of Candelaria.

We went back to pounding in the pilings with the hand-powered pile driver. The engineers seemed to regard this bridge as a showpiece on display to the town. When the main structure across the river was in place, Lieutenant Miyosato supervised construction of heavy side rails on posts set into the concrete at the edge of the bridge. The rails were eight-by-eight timbers, beautifully finished by precise trimming with an adze and smoothing with wooden planes and polishing. Finally, Japanese characters were engraved on the inner surface of the railing at each end of the bridge, giving the date and the circumstances as well as the unit name. With the engineers, we had begun to feel that a bridge should be a work of art as well as a utilitarian river crossing. Captain Wakamori and the mayor cooperated in a brief ceremony. We listened to short speeches in Japanese and Tagalog, understanding mainly the gestures. Some of us got a sip of the saki that was drunk to christen the bridge.

In the middle of September when the bridge-building jobs were finished, the engineers trucked us back to Calauan. On the way Sergeant Teramura ordered a halt in San Pablo. The town was full of Japanese soldiers and officers wearing polished boots and carrying swords with jeweled buttons that indicated samurai ancestors. Three-Star Private Nikki herded some of us over to a market shop and, grinning happily, bought us fruit and sweet cakes. He didn't salute or bow to any of the officers. Corporal Ishitani had told me that in China Nikki had been "dai ichi heitai" ("the number one soldier") in Captain Wakamori's command. Ishitani had pointed to little citation marks on Nikki's collar. But none of the engineers seemed to pay much attention to the rigid military courtesy with other Japanese units, and as elite combat troops they seemed to get away with it. We felt nervous.

30

CABANATUAN PRISON CAMP NUMBER ONE

*B*ACK AT CALAUAN we stacked tools in boxes to be trucked away, and we cleaned up the buildings and the yards of the buildings where we lived. A week of rest was a gift to us and the combat engineers for a job well done. In Calauan our Filipino friends openly gave us a supply of cigars and cigarillos. When we were finally loaded into two Japanese trucks for the trip north to Manila, Captain Wakamori gave us each a cigarillo and stood in the square waving a handkerchief after us until we were out of sight. Dr. Marfori, Dr. de Guzman, Maria Ravelo, Dr. Schultz, and many others waved us off too.

We were driven back to the shoe factory where we had spent a night on the way south to Calauan. We loafed for two days. Our guards were Sergeant Teramura, Corporal Ishitani, and Three-Star Private Nikki. They talked and loafed with us and made sure we were well fed. Early on the morning of September 20, 1942, we were roused, fed, counted, and trucked to the town of Cabanatuan. In the market our escorts ordered us to get out with our duffel bags, and they bought us pineapples, papayas, mongo beans, sausages, field corn, cigarillos, and handfuls of limes. They had the Filipinos stuff our duffel bags. The Filipinos, as though we were old friends, stuffed even more food into our bags. Ishitani was grinning from ear to ear the whole time. "Carpentoors very good," he said.

At last Teramura ordered us back into the truck, and we were driven the six miles to Cabanatuan Prison Camp. We piled out with our new store of food and found ourselves in front of the main gate of the prison camp of barbed wire, towers, and old barracks. Japanese guards and two American marine majors approached from the camp.

149

One of the marine majors, Major Bradley, stood to one side and waited. The other, speaking fluent Japanese, joined them in starting to search us.

Then Sergeant Teramura stepped in between these shakedown artists and burst into an angry barrage of orders. The guards and the marine with them backed away, cowed by the elite quality of the combat engineers. Sergeant Teramura beckoned forward Corporal Ishitani and Three-Star Private Nikki. On each duffel bag they tied an identification card stamped with the combat engineers' company "chop."

Then we had an awkward and sad little ceremony. We stiffly bowed, and each of the combat engineers shook hands with each of us. Sergeant Teramura repeated the advice he had given me weeks ago when we were sitting out the rain in the shelter of the nipa hut: "Do as told, learn language."

The Japanese camp guards and their marine major friend had retreated to the camp gate. Now we were motioned closer to that side of the road by Major Bradley. "Guard your sabisu [gift] with your life," he said softly, with a warning nod toward the Cabanatuan guards—or was it toward the other marine major?

And then we saw and smelled what he had waved us aside for. The burial detail was coming out of the hospital on the opposite side of the street. Four men carried each hospital litter bearing a naked, almost skeletal corpse. Thirty-one litters passed by. The bearers were almost as thin as the corpses they bore.

We walked through the gates still under the watch of Sergeant Teramura, Corporal Ishitani, and Three-Star Private Nikki. We waved and clutched our duffel bags to our shoulders. Inside we saw some horyo standing near the fence. Two of the Japanese cooks had crossed the road with a huge dishpan. They stopped at the fence and threw out animal entrails. The thin horyo began to squabble over them. The entrails, we learned, were those of a brahma steer slaughtered for the Japanese kitchen. As we turned back to Major Bradley, we were frozen in a new seriousness. We looked back toward the gate and saw the three combat engineers still watching us. Major Bradley assigned us to bahays, barracks. One by one we carried our duffel bags off to our assigned places. It was the last time for many months that we would look on any Japanese as friends or regret seeing the last of them.

The Cabanatuan camp was horrifyingly like some of our memories of O'Donnell. Many of the men were walking skeletons, and some were misshapen, with testicles so enlarged that the men were bent over carrying them in their hands. Those with dysentery shuffled along half-covered with feces. One friend's face was so swollen with beriberi that I did not recognize him until he spoke to me. He was a member of the 194th, and he soon died in the zero ward.

On my way to my assigned bahay I was passing one of the rice kitchens when I suddenly saw the familiar tough face of Tex Simmons. One of the top soldiers of the 194th, Tex had swum to Corregidor rather than surrender on Bataan. He had fought in the beach defenses there until he was wounded in the leg. He had eventually been put in Bilibid Prison and from there sent to Cabanatuan, where he had become a mess sergeant.

"Fitz, I need another rice cook. Stow your gear here in back. I bunk there, and I'll arrange for you to bunk here too." Tex went on a mile a minute about how bad things were in Cabanatuan Prison Camp. "Look, Fitz, this place is rough, but you'll be better off with some work—give you something to do, so you don't get feeling down. I'll work you some—noon to noon and then twenty-four off, just like in a regular mess hall. Want you bunking down here to start the fire early. What have you got in this barracks bag?" He was helping me carry it inside, around the raised hearth and to the back of the building, where he set the bag down on a big table and pointed to one of the bunks.

In a few minutes he had settled me in, taken me to my assigned bahay, arranged with the barracks leader for me to sleep at the kitchen, checked in with the mess officer for his kitchen, and told me about the camp customs and what had happened to our friends, mostly either in bad shape or dead, and Colonel Miller: "The Old Man is here, and he does his best to keep track of everyone and keep them going." For the next week I worked for Tex in the kitchen and had a bad attack of my chronic malaria. Tex spoon-fed me for a couple of days, and I felt lucky indeed between the chills and fever.

At Cabanatuan what we were fed and how we were fed was our most important concern. The food for each day was issued after supper the previous evening, so bunking in the kitchen involved not only starting the fires early but also guarding the food.

Every morning at 4 A.M. those on duty began to build and light the fires in the raised hearths in the kitchen. We put on the big pots filled with rice and water. The main dish each morning was lugao, a soft, pasty rice gruel, often with worms in it. On fires outside we heated

"Quan and Quaning," a drawing by Ben Steele. As the prisoners understood it, the word "quan" meant anything edible in the Philippine language. Eventually all prisoners obtained or made a can in which to collect and cook edible items (weeds, insects, snakes, etc.). The container became their "quan can," a very valuable possession.

up the unsweetened green tea and a sort of vegetable soup. The usual base for the soup was made of the heads cut from fish served to the Japanese garrison the previous supper. We eagerly devoured the fish-head remnants, bones and all. The vegetables in the soup were few: camote vines, whistleweed, and pechay. On occasion the soup contained eggplant. Once a week we were issued carabao meat, an ounce per man, and once a month we received 50 eggs per 500 men. These stocks went into soups.

Tex's kitchen fed three bahays, each with about 100 men. Usually, the first to come in the morning were men on the wood-gathering detail. Every day this detail went out with axes, saws, and machetes to cut trees blown down during typhoon season and also green trees. Every day a battered old truck delivered the trunks and large branches to each kitchen, and a chopping detail cut them up. The mixture of dry and green wood burned very hot. The smoke escaped through the nipa roof and out of the sides, which opened the full length of the kitchen. The pots were black with soot.

"Noon Fight Over Food," a drawing by Ben Steele.

"Cabanatuan Beef," a drawing by Ben Steele.

At noon we served rice, tea, and the vegetable soup. For supper we served dry rice, tea, the soup, and often a piece of camote, the sweet-potato–like vegetable common in the Philippines. Tex saved the crusted rice scraped from the pots. The prisoners who suffered the most from dysentery preferred this dry, crusted rice, and Tex saw that they got it.

When a man was too sick to come to the rice line, a friend brought his mess kit to take his food back. Sometimes after the man in the bahay had died, the friend ate both rations for a day or two before reporting the death. Sometimes a man was assumed dead and came out of his coma as the burial detail began to shovel dirt onto him. Some were undoubtedly buried alive. One man who survived such a premature and fortunately uncompleted burial was asked how he had felt. He said, "I felt this was no place for me."

31

BREAKOUT

ALL THE PRISONERS captured in the Philippines in 1942 were aware of their rights under the Geneva Convention, or they were soon informed of these rights by their fellow prisoners. To attempt to escape was the prisoner's duty, under U.S. Army and Navy regulations and according to the Geneva Convention. There ought to be no reprisal other than solitary confinement or a cut in rations, either against the soldier escaping if he was caught or against his fellows left behind in the prison camp. But all the prisoners were also soon aware that Japan, as well as Russia, had refused to ratify the Geneva Convention of 1929. Japan objected to clauses such as the right of a prisoner to attempt escape and the requirement that prison camps be inspected by the International Red Cross.

To discourage escapes the Japanese used a simple system, explained by the Japanese authorities in each camp and by American barracks leaders at least every week. For any man who escaped or attempted to escape, his group of ten blood brothers would be executed. Sometimes the definition of blood brothers seemed to be you, the prisoner, and the four men who slept on either side of you. Sometimes it was a previously designated group of ten. Needless to say, everyone quickly developed a concern for the whereabouts of his nine blood brothers.

In the Philippines, with an enormously sympathetic population and large areas of the country held by guerrilla bands, escape was possible and tempting. Despite the system of reprisal, some men tried to escape. For them escape may have seemed the only way to survive. Others rationalized that the Soldier's Code of Conduct established their legal duty to escape. The punishment inflicted on their blood brothers served as a warning to those who remained.

One of the best-known escape attempts in the Philippines occurred at Cabanatuan on September 27, 1942. On that evening the fall monsoons were blowing steady rain in from the China Sea. On the perimeter of the camp outside the wire, Japanese guards walked their posts or stood on the tall guard towers. Inside the wire, war prisoners also walked their posts as interior guards. The American headquarters in camp was compelled by the Japanese to provide these guards. The Japanese had another method to make escape morally difficult for prisoners. If an interior guard allowed an escape through his post, he, as well as the blood brothers of the escapees, would pay with his life.

As I remember it, Mario Tonelli, a former football player from Notre Dame, was on duty as an interior guard. At the end of his post the wide, shallow drainage ditch from the latrines ran north under the barbed-wire fence past one of the guard towers. Two other prisoners stopped by the drainage ditch to urinate. Because of malnutrition and disease, most prisoners had to urinate about once an hour. Using the ditch was handier than going all the way to the latrine, particularly in the rain. The streams of urine landed on the head and shoulders of someone crawling in the ditch. He complained vociferously. The guard, Tonelli, took a look into the ditch and saw three men: Lieutenant Colonel Lloyd W. Biggs, Lieutenant Colonel E. C. Breitung, and navy Lieutenant Roy Gilbert.

These three officers had not made the march out of Bataan to O'Donnell but had been captured on Corregidor, and they may not have believed that the Japanese would execute their 27 blood brothers, although it is difficult to understand such naiveté. At any rate, they had collected medicine and money. Lieutenant Gilbert, a civil engineer, was supposed to be familiar with the country, and they hoped to find the guerrillas.

Tonelli told them to go back to their quarters. He reminded them that otherwise their 27 blood brothers would be executed. They ordered him to leave them alone and crawled farther down the ditch. Tonelli said that it would be his neck too if they escaped, and he leaped into the ditch to grab them. The altercation grew louder and louder, perhaps because Colonel Biggs was somewhat deaf and short-tempered. A Japanese guard on the outside heard them and fired a shot or two to attract attention, and immediately more interior guards and American officers from nearby bahays came stumbling out into the slippery, rain-swept darkness.

The next morning in the rice line we were all reconstructing the event. We could see how far the three men had crawled in the drainage

Torture of American war prisoners, Cabanatuan Prison Camp, 1942. Artist of drawing unknown.

ditch: about 200 yards, with another 100 to go. Some said that a tower sentry had put a spotlight on them and that he was the one who had fired the warning shots.

We heard similar stories about the confrontation between the escapees and Lieutenant Colonel Mori, the Japanese camp commandant. He accused them of "failure to cooperate" and "bad faith." After arguing with Mori about the right of a prisoner to escape, Biggs apparently lost his temper and asserted that Mori would be brought to justice after the war.

At this point no mercy would be shown to the three men. Colonel Mori had been insulted in front of his own men. He ordered discipline for them. They were beaten thoroughly. The next morning they were tied up outside the Japanese headquarters and beaten through the day and into the second night. On the following morning they were stripped and lashed to the fence posts of the main gate of the camp. Any Filipino passing through the gate was required to beat each of the three men or suffer a beating himself. The Japanese guards, of course, contributed freely.

That night the three prisoners, still without food or water, were left hanging from the posts during a typhoon. The tropical wind and rain slashed at them for hours. The next day they were taken down, driven off in a truck, and shot. Colonel Miller writes that while he was at Cabanatuan, no escapee succeeded. They were all brought back to be paraded with a sign announcing that they had tried to escape, and they were all executed.

This escape attempt occurred one week after I arrived at Cabanatuan. Tex Simmons and I had finished cleaning up after the evening meal, and I was in my bunk in the back of the kitchen. Although the rice kitchen was not far from headquarters, neither of us took any notice of the commotion. Such disturbances were fairly common. The next morning when I was serving the men in the rice line, I heard the constant discussion about the escape attempt. Then I saw the prisoners tied to their posts outside the guard headquarters. Smugglers were often beaten, and it was still raining. We talked about the preparations these men had made to escape and about the punishment of the officers in the escapees' bahay. They were locked in, with the side panels shut, with only a pail for a toilet, and with even less food than usual, in the heat and moisture of the rainy season. In this case the blood brother groups weren't gathered for execution. In two other incidents in July 1942, Earl G. Smith and Howell A. Emley, both members of the 194th Tank Battalion, were executed as blood brothers of would-be escapees. They were on different details at the time, outside of Cabanatuan.

On another occasion two delirious men, near death from malaria and other diseases, wandered aimlessly away from the hospital into the high cogon grass. Their blood brother groups had been summoned to be shot by the time the sick men were found. One had lain down in the grass to die, clutching a partly eaten rat. The other was dead, discovered by searchers from the hospital.

In 1943 at Cabanatuan a red-headed American soldier was regularly trading with one of the Japanese guards while he was walking his post. When the Japanese officer of the day caught them in the act, the guard grabbed the soldier and claimed that he had been trying to escape.

The Japanese knew otherwise, so blood brothers were not summoned, but the American prisoner was executed. In plain sight of us, he was offered a cigarette and then a blindfold. He refused them both with contempt. Lieutenant Henry G. Lee remembered him in a poem, "An Execution," which ends,

> What matter why he stood facing the gun?
> We saw a nation's pride there in the sun.

The moral problem remains to this day. The Soldier's Code of Conduct, adopted on July 5, 1955, rests on traditions from the Revolutionary War: loyalty to one's country, loyalty to one's fellow soldiers, the duty to obey one's officers, the duty not to surrender while one has the ability to resist, the duty to escape if one is captured. The Geneva Convention laid a basis in international law for the actions of a war prisoner and his captors. In the Soldier's Code, signed by President Eisenhower, Article III says, "I will make every effort to escape and aid others to escape." But Article IV adds, "If I become a prisoner of war, I will keep faith with my fellow prisoners. I will give no information nor take part in any action which might be harmful to my comrades."

The soldier's training manual comments on the relationship between Article IV of the Soldier's Code and Article 105 of the Uniform Code of Military Justice, which forbids "all unauthorized conduct by a prisoner of war that would improve his condition while making conditions worse for his fellow prisoners." The training manual adds, "However, escape, which results in closer confinement or other measures against fellow prisoners still in the hands of the enemy, is not an offense under this article." I do not know the source of this extraordinary exception, which is not stated in Article 105 of the Uniform Code of Military Justice.

Implicit in the Soldier's Code is an unresolved conflict between Article III and Article IV. If escaping means the death of one's fellow prisoners, does the legal duty to escape take precedence over the moral commitment not to "take part in any action which might be harmful to my comrades"? Might the "other measures against fellow prisoners still in the hands of the enemy" be so severe that one ought not to escape?

By April 1943 American prisoners in Cabanatuan understood clearly what reprisals would be taken for an escape. Once the Japanese had established the blood brother system, any prisoner should have

have been able to judge for himself that escape was morally wrong. In Cabanatuan during late 1942 and early 1943 the chaplains and senior officers discussed this dilemma of a soldier's legal duty to try to escape and his moral commitment to his fellow prisoners. They agreed that the moral obligation took precedence.

32

HEROES OF CABANATUAN

IN JUNE AND JULY 1942 the unfinished Philippine army camp at Cabanatuan had been converted to a prison camp, and exhausted, starved, and diseased survivors of Camp O'Donnell had been moved in with prisoners from Corregidor, dazed from their surrender. In those two months, when I had been with the bridge-building detail, nearly 2,000 prisoners died. In August 1942 conditions had improved, with tiny amounts of carabao meat, a few bananas, and a few cucumbers, and food occasionally smuggled into the camp also helped reduce the death rate. But the prisoners slowly lost weight and succumbed to diseases from malnutrition and the flies, mosquitoes, fungi, and vermin that feasted on us.

One day Tex and I visited our close friend Bill Monroe in the hospital. First we applied to American headquarters. The duty officer gave us a stick with a white rag attached. We went to the gate and bowed to the guards. They allowed us to cross the road into the hospital compound, where we handed the stick to the guards. When we left, we went through the procedure again like children getting hall passes in an old-fashioned school.

Tex led me among the hospital bahays to the zero ward, where men were lying nearly naked on the floor or the ground, without beds, cots, or even mats. Some had bits of burlap. The place stank. Tex and I didn't look at each other. Monroe had sores, and his bones were sharp against his skin. Tex lit a cigarillo for him and put it between his lips. Monroe smiled and said, "Thanks," and his eyes rolled back. Tex had been trying to get Monroe to come back to the work side of the camp, where he could help him fight for his life. Two days later Monroe died.

I remember Monroe coming out of Bataan on the Hike. At one halt he began to pick his teeth with a twig. He looked around and grinned and said, "Anyone want half of my steak?" Some of the men had called him Billy the Kid. I asked him if he minded if I called him that, and he replied in his soft, deliberate, southern drawl, "Call me William the Boy."

The malodorous straddle-trench latrines were open, and the overflow meandered along shallow ditches to sump holes within and just outside the barbed-wire fence. Flies, maggots, and other insects bred and swarmed over everything. One had to battle them to eat rice. The Japanese, across the road, hated the huge, swollen bluebottle flies. They gave a small bun to each man who killed 100 of them, reminding me of the gopher skins I turned in for a nickel's bounty in the 1930s. Ninety percent of the 6,000 prisoners in Cabanatuan had dysentery. The disease cramped and dehydrated prisoners already weakened by malaria and the whole complex of the diseases of malnutrition— beriberi, scurvy, pellagra, and jaundice. Those weakened by dysentery did not always reach the straddle trenches in time, and some fell into the trenches. Some men wore burlap skirts and squatted wherever they happened to be. Some crawled under a bahay to linger awhile in a coma and die.

These conditions were greatly improved by Lieutenant Colonel Fred Saint, Captain John Presnell, Major Lew Barbour, Warrant Officer Garfallo, and a few others, who designed, dug, and built a complete sanitation system for 6,000 men. Saint, Presnell, and Barbour were all West Pointers and army engineers. They went into the festering sump holes to dig them out and send the night soil off to the farm area. They planned and constructed the ditches. They built a complete system of locks to move water to new field latrines, flush them out, and carry the sewage to sump holes. They cut steel drums in half and joined them to make troughs. They built high wooden boxes for 16-hole field latrines. The troughs passed underneath, and the water that accumulated in a whole steel drum was automatically tripped to flush out each trough. They built nipa-palm roofs over each unit of 16 seats. At last those with dysentery could sit down. Each morning a small detail went to every latrine and made sure it was clean and working and that all the locks were properly flushed out.

This work, accomplished between late October and the middle of December 1942, without help from the Japanese, was one of the primary factors in reducing the death rate throughout the camp. These men, often up to their necks in sewage and with grins on their faces were, as one man commented, "brilliant and covered with shit." These men were worthy of the highest praise, the highest decorations our country can award.

In November 1942 men were shipped to Davao, Japan, Korea, and Manchuria. Tex Simmons was transported to Manchuria about the second week of November, and his kitchen was closed. I was moved to a bahay in Group I, in the corner of camp near the platform of the entertainment area. Even with the influx of men from the closing of Cabanatuan Prison Camp Number Three, there were now fewer prisoners in the compound.

Colonel Miller was shipped to Japan at that time. He had been the backbone for all of us in the 194th Tank Battalion. In the evenings in prison camp some of us visited him at the colonels' barracks. Although he no longer had direct command over us, he was always able to cheer up discouraged prisoners. He became very thin. On the evening he left for Japan, the men from our battalion lined up, shook his hand, and saluted. Albin Milstien from Mahnomen, Minnesota, was almost too weak to stand, but he stepped forward and insisted that Colonel Miller accept his gift of a can of sardines. Albin died of starvation a couple of weeks later.

In September 1945, after our release, I met Colonel Miller in the repatriation area at Muntinlupa. He was chomping on a cheroot. We gathered around him, and he asked how each of us was and what he could do to help. After the war he became the commander of the Minnesota American Legion. He was a strong advocate of military preparedness and was the first director of the state's civil defense. In 1949 he published *Bataan Uncensored*, a frank account of his war experiences in the Philippines and Japan. Only recently has his book received the historical attention it deserves. Colonel Miller was greatly troubled over the loss of men in his battalion, especially when soon after the war he addressed a reunion of the 194th Tank Battalion in Brainerd, Minnesota, where 25 percent of the audience were surviving members of the battalion and the rest were Gold Star mothers. He died on February 20, 1959.

One morning in late November 1942 a smartly uniformed team of Japanese doctors inspected the camp. The leader was free of the swagger that afflicted most of the Japanese officers. In clear but stilted English he said to our commanding officer, Major Thompson Brooke Maury, "We must have more protein in your mess."

Soon a small herd of carabao was driven to the camp. The Japanese had taken them from the Filipinos, paying with the inflated occupation scrip. For a cowherd, the Japanese chose a remarkable prisoner known as Old Kliatchko. He had received his early education at a rabbinical seminary in Warsaw. He came to the United States to escape a pogrom, and as a volunteer in the First World War he fought at the Argonne Forest. He stayed in the army engineers after the war and retired in the Philippines. He married a Filipino and became a farmer in Bulacan province. At the start of the war he sailed alone in a small barca down the west coast of Luzon at night, and at Bataan he volunteered in the engineers. He was 62 years old. Now with his worn army campaign hat and a large, gnarled stick, he gently prodded the carabao to pasture each morning and brought them back at sunset, singing in a sure and powerful bass the songs of Isaiah and the lamentations of Jeremiah.

Near the middle of December 1942, after many rebuffs, the Red Cross in Manila finally received permission to ship in medicine, especially quinine and sulfathiazole. In early February 1943 ten doctors and 20 corpsmen arrived from the closed Cabanatuan Prison Camp Number Three. Morale improved, thanks to the dedicated medical officers, who encouraged the sick to grow gardens, attend lectures, join singing groups, participate in games and handicrafts, and build Carabao Wallow, a sort of sidewalk cafe. After a while the prisoners were making wooden shoes, getting their hair cut, and patching their clothes.

33

THE MASS OF THE BLUE MOON

WHEN WE HAD cleaned up the rice kitchen one evening back in October 1942, just after my attack of malaria, Tex said, "Let's walk on over and listen to this group that's going to sing."

"Who is directing them? Are they any good?" I asked, interested, as Tex knew I would be.

"A guy named Captain Childers, Fifty-Seventh Philippine Scouts. They're not too bad. Maybe they'll let you sing along with them."

We found a large group of prisoners sitting cross-legged on the ground in front of a makeshift platform of wood scrounged from the Japanese. We stood on the edge of the crowd and listened to about 25 men on the platform singing old army favorites—Stephen Foster songs, spirituals, and sentimental songs familiar to the audience.

I moved forward a bit, and someone made room for me. He was Sergeant Gus Sayre, a corpsman with the 31st Infantry. We talked about the music, and I learned that he had a degree in music from Stanford University. I told him about studying voice at the College of St. Thomas in St. Paul, where I had been president of the glee club, a position for which I had been thoroughly razzed at Coughlin's, the local pub. We exchanged ideas about improving the singers on the platform. A tall, spare lieutenant colonel overheard us and said, "Why don't you two come and see me tomorrow. I'm Colonel Wilson."

So the next day Gus Sayre waited at Tex's kitchen until I was through working. At the small sawali shack that served as entertainment or morale headquarters, Colonel O. O. Wilson, known as Zero, and his assistant Lieutenant Al Manning, known as Harvard Al, were waiting for us.

"Now you two were criticizing last night," Colonel Wilson said in a very cool, very soft Texas drawl. "And you ought to have something positive to offer before you go talking that way. Captain Childers never did want the job to begin with. Why don't you two men take over?"

And before we knew it, Gus and I were forming a glee club, in addition to our regular jobs. All rehearsals were after hours. Later I learned that Colonel Wilson had asked about both of us in advance and had made certain we knew how to run a glee club.

About a week after we had started recruiting the best voices, we acquired another job. Chaplain Tiffany and Father Tom Secina cornered Gus and me after a rehearsal. Would we like to form a choir for the camp church services?

"One of Captain Childers's problems was that he didn't have any music," Gus told them. "What could we do about that?"

Chaplain Tiffany said, "I have one standard army hymnal. Father Secina, couldn't you promote something from Father Buttenbruch in Manila?"

"I think so," Father Secina said. "You could use a little field organ, too. Do you know Fran Boyer of the Fourth Marines? He told me once that he knew something about arranging music."

Before long we had 24 men representing all ranks and all branches of the service. We looked forward to rehearsals. This period of my prison life, when I worked with this choral group, was the most bearable and rewarding. Along with regular camp work, it kept me occupied almost completely. I made friendships that I still cherish, and I've never worked with a more dedicated or enthusiastic group.

We almost foundered for lack of paper to copy music on, but Major Maury, the American camp commander, gave us paper labels salvaged by the can-flattening detail. The Japanese had ordered us to flatten and bale all empty cans, and they sent them to Japan to be recycled.

Fran Boyer worked out arrangements on the field organ for two-part and then three-part harmony, and by 1944 we were working on four-part harmony. He would write out a copy on the back of a can label, and the other prisoners wrote three can-label copies for each voice for the choral group. At first Fran worked on fairly simple favorites to sing for concerts. Then we progressed to choral music that we could sing as a glee club and as a choir.

Chaplain Tiffany and Father Secina had another request in early November 1942. What about a program of Christmas carols and music for a Christmas mass? Father Secina triumphantly produced a small St. Gregory hymnal.

Major Thompson Brooke Maury, American camp commander at Cabanatuan Prison Camp. This photograph taken shortly before the war appeared in *Gardens, Houses and People* magazine.

"Do you have permission from the Japanese?" I asked skeptically.

"Well, no, we don't," said Chaplain Tiffany, "but one Major Thompson Brooke Maury the Seventh is working up a campaign for us." Major Maury came from an illustrious southern family, and some men joked about it as a sign of their liking for him.

About two weeks before Christmas, Major Maury happily informed us that the Japanese had authorized a Christmas Eve midnight mass. "The Cabanatuan ecumenical movement has had its first great success," he reported, "or, rather, the Episcopal member has done his part. Now it's up to you chaplains and the choir people." Major Maury became an invaluable member of our choral group.

Despite the many illnesses that plagued us, we went to work with even more enthusiasm. From the army hymnal we transcribed Christmas carols in three-part harmony. From the St. Gregory hymnal we transcribed the *Missa de Angelis* in single voice. We later substituted the Kyrie, Gloria, Sanctus, and Agnus Dei from Montani's *Missa Brevis*, a simple and melodious mass.

On the raised platform in the entertainment area, Colonel David Babcock fashioned a simple altar, which was later used for all church services. He also talked with us and constructed a sawali sound backboard for the choir. The Japanese allowed Father Buttenbruch to bring vestments into camp for the priests. As Christmas Eve approached, we all felt an air of hope and optimism. We had reason: the carabao meat in the stew, food for sale in the commissary, and the decline of the death rate.

Long before midnight, prisoners of all faiths assembled near the platform with the altar. Around 11 P.M. the glee club and choir began to sing Christmas carols. The audience joined us softly. Then some of the chaplains spoke briefly. A gentle wind continued to blow from the west, and the full moon rose higher. Major Maury announced that on that day only five prisoners had died, and there was silence, a silent prayer.

At midnight we began the very formal high mass. The choir stood in front of the backboard, using the four candles that we had been allowed for reading our music. Gus, at the diminutive field organ, was so afflicted with scurvy that when he sang, his mouth and lips looked like an open sore. As we began to sing "O Sanctissima" in four-four time, the priests, in the rich vestments from Manila, approached the altar. As I directed the choir, I felt that I had never seen such dedicated and expectant faces, in the light of the moon and the candles. Just then someone near the edge of the huge gathering shouted at the top of his lungs, "Kiotsuke!" ("Attention!")

We all froze. Was there trouble, an escape? That command meant the Japanese were in camp, and they seldom entered the work area. Now the Japanese camp commander and all his staff, wearing no side arms, filed to an open space near the platform and sat on the grass cross-legged and with folded arms, intent and respectful.

The solemn high mass began. Father Stanley Riley was the celebrant. Father William Cummings served as deacon and Father John Wilson as subdeacon. Father Secina was master of ceremonies, signaling the choir and helping the serving priests change vestments when necessary. Father John McDonald gave the brief homily. Father James O'Brien sang with the choir. We sang the complete common of the mass (the parts that never change—the Kyrie, Gloria, Credo, Sanctus, and Agnus Dei) and plain-chanted the proper (the parts that change according to the season of the church calendar—the Introit, Gradual, Offertory, and Communion).

The gentle wind almost ceased, and the two candles for reading the mass book never flickered. The full moon shone so brightly that the candles were not really needed. Angus Duncan, a miner from Scotland and an old dobie in the Philippines, said later, "I've lived here most of my life, and at Christmastide I've never witnessed such a stilling of the winds and such brightness of the moon. It won't happen again in a blue moon."

At the end of the mass the choir sang "Oh Come, All Ye Faithful" as the priests in measured pace left the altar and passed behind the altar stage. The Japanese commander and his staff filed toward the gate to their area of the camp. Looking to the horizon, I saw the bright Southern Cross.

34

THE MAYOR OF BILIBID

*I*N THE DAYS before Pearl Harbor, to bring the 194th Tank Battalion up to wartime strength at Angel Island in San Francisco Bay, new soldiers were assigned to the battalion. Some were volunteers from various west-coast units, and some were shanghais, men who were ordered to "volunteer." In the mid-afternoon sunshine of September 9, 1941, at the embarkation pier at Fort Mason, one of these men sitting on his barracks bag had in his drooping brown eyes a doleful look from the pain of a hangover. His name was José Sanchez.

Up the gangplank we went into the *President Coolidge*, which was still outfitted as a luxury liner except for the four-decker bunks in the holds. A year later the *President Coolidge* would leave her bones on the teeth of Guadalcanal. We were shoveled below, and José and I were side by side in the second tier of folding bunks amidships. We decided to sack out before chow time. I went solidly to sleep. A long last night out in Chinatown with Phil Brain, Bill McKeon, and Tex Simmons had caught up with me. I had buttoned down my shirt-pocket flap over an expensive Parker pen and pencil set that my mother had sent as a reminder to write as often as I could.

I woke up almost late for chow and with no pen and pencil set. José Sanchez was not in the next bunk. I boiled upstairs onto the deck and, brushing my way through the men, finally ran down my quarry. There was José in KP whites, shooting craps with a huge stack of money in front of him. No apology: José handed me the pen and pencil set and a $5 bill. I had unwittingly staked him.

In those days a private received $21 a month. I sent $10 to St. Paul, Minnesota, to pay the monthly installment on my piano. I took the $5 and the pen and pencil set. There was nothing to say. By the time we reached Manila, Jo had so much money he was wearing an improvised money belt, and most of his money was in the purser's safe.

Eventually, the purser had to ask José when he needed smaller bills for change.

José had cagily volunteered to work in the ship's galley for the civilian crew, because he was an excellent cook and because the job would give him the run of the ship, would keep him well fed and close to the supplies of liquor, and would allow him time for his favorite pastime, gambling at craps or poker. José found a way to help the men who could not face the smell of the chow line without seasickness. These men went to the ship's fantail at night in the cool salt air, and he brought them platters of special food such as roasted chickens.

During those days aboard ship I asked Jo to teach me some of his skills at dice. He replied, "Kid, this game is not for you." He told me not to waste my money on the horses at the Santa Anita racetrack in Manila, because "they're all doctored." Jo had sensed I would never make a sharp gambler. I never tried my luck at dice or horses after that.

In late September we entered Manila Bay. At Fort Stotsenburg, next to Clark Field, José and I were in the same tent. Next morning at reveille José was absent, and Captain Burke, the commander of our Company A, found him in the off-limits village of Sapangbato, where Jo and a soldier named Conroy were happily drinking rum and Coke. Captain Burke made José and Conroy run quick-time back to camp, in front of his jeep down the middle of the dusty road and right through the company street to the orderly room. José felt he had been humiliated more than was necessary for the offense, and he never quite forgave Captain Burke. The first sergeant gave him a week's punishment on KP.

Jo was such a capable KP that he was made a cook, and soon the food improved so much that the noncommissioned officers, who had been eating at the noncoms' club, joined us in the regular mess hall. José was made acting mess sergeant, and eventually he was entrusted with ordering all the company food supplies from Manila. He personally assisted in unloading each truck. He rarely left the mess hall. José was just a touch drunk all the time. He was having a good supply of lemon extract delivered to supplement the local supplies of beer and the Spanish gin.

One morning as he emerged unsteadily from the mess hall, José found his friend Pedro López, the company barber, preparing to shave the first sergeant, already lathered and with a hot towel over his eyes. Unsober as he was, Jo immediately became the master barber. He plucked the straight-edged razor from Pedro's hand, delicately removed the hot towel, and with the utmost dexterity and perfect economy of motion, he shaved the first sergeant. He didn't nick him once. Everyone in the company street, seeing the straight razor and knowing Jo's explosive temper, were helpless with strangled howls of laughter.

The first sergeant finally realized who was shaving him and, seeing José's condition, let out a roar that must have been heard in Manila. Charged with being drunk on duty, Jo was court-martialed and sentenced to 30 days in the battalion guardhouse. His sentence would have been more severe, but at the last second of the court-martial, he let slip that the first sergeant had called him "a dirty Mexican son of a bitch." The first sergeant promptly received an open reprimand from the presiding colonel, and Jo, with a reduced sentence, was taken off to the guardhouse.

The sergeant of the guard was Ken Porwoll. José requested emergency medical treatment, in the form of a few bottles of beer. Ken, recalling the roast chicken served at night on the fantail of the *President Coolidge*, provided José with a supply of beer whenever he came on duty. Each Saturday afternoon Jo asked to be taken to the Fort Stotsenburg post office to send home the money he'd won from the battalion guards during the week.

Someone conceived the bright idea that Jo ought to be given some work while he was serving his sentence. One morning a truck, a driver, a guard, and Jo were sent to the gravel pit. José was to shovel the truck full of gravel. About mid-afternoon the officer of the day decided that the truck had been gone too long. He found the guard putting the last few shovelfuls in the truck, while José took his ease in the shade of the truck with the guard's rifle resting across his lap. The guard had accepted Jo's offer of 20 pesos to do the work. An immediate decision came down from battalion headquarters that Jo should be confined. Major Miller remarked drily, "Not without cause."

War broke out about the time José was released. The newly arrived commander of Tank Group Number One, Colonel James R. N. Weaver, requested each of the two tank battalions under his command to send him men to staff his headquarters. José was asked to volunteer from Company A.

One afternoon when the 194th Tank Battalion was helping cover the withdrawal of the Philippine army from Lingayen Gulf to Bataan in December 1941, up from the south came a half-track with an identifying one star. It was the recently promoted General Weaver. Standing up behind the general was José Sanchez. General Weaver found Colonel Miller and thanked him for assigning to his headquarters such a well-qualified man as José. Not only was Jo a good man with the machine gun on the half-track but he also cooked excellently for General Weaver, finding chickens, canned hams, fresh vegetables, and after-dinner liqueurs. We already knew about Jo's ability to acquire wayward chickens along the roads. Colonel Miller was grimly amused by the general's praise. Later he commented, "They deserve each other."

But the colonel also respected Jo's abilities as a tough soldier, despite his soft, plump appearance. He aimed a machine gun with as much skill as he threw dice. Jo, in turn, had a high regard for the colonel and always felt he belonged with the 194th Tank Battalion.

One morning shortly after his visit with General Weaver, José joined the crew of one of the machine-gun half-tracks under fire in a delaying action against a Japanese spearhead mobile unit. A Japanese 12.5 millimeter shell punctured the half-track, ricocheted off the inside of the armor, and hit Jo's right leg between the knee and the ankle.

In the outdoor hospital on the southern end of Bataan, he and Ken Porwoll were patients together. Jo had lost not only a foot but all his money. Ken searched his pockets and came up with 53 centavos, about 25 cents, as José's stake for a crap game. Two days later Jo came back to Ken's cot, handed him $100, and said, "Our partnership is dissolved." Soon Ken went back to his job commanding a tank in Company A.

One day Jo came stumping along the jungle trail to ask Colonel Miller for permission to return to duty with his old battalion, if only as a guard. In the hospital he had carved himself an artificial limb out of bamboo. Colonel Miller thanked José but sent him back to the hospital for further treatment.

Months after the surrender of Bataan and Corregidor, in October 1942 Ken Porwoll was one of a large group of prisoners about to be shipped to Japan. He was so sick from malnutrition, malaria, dysentery, and jaundice that he could not march the six miles from camp to the railroad station in the town of Cabanatuan. He was thrown into the back of a truck with some other prisoners and taken to the railroad, stuffed into a boxcar, and sent to Manila to be unloaded at Pier 7. Ken was barely able to move, and when the Japanese ship left, Ken and another American soldier were found lying in a corner of the pier.

Two Japanese guards made some Filipinos load the semiconscious Americans into one of their calesas and haul them up the Avenida Rizal to Bilibid Prison. The Japanese guards dumped their prisoners on the street in front of the prison. They told the prison guards to open the gates, and they heaved them in.

Standing to one side of the stone entrance of Bilibid, José recognized Ken and followed the procession to the place where Ken and the other soldier were laid down. Ken later recalled, "So weak I can't stand, I can't even crawl, and I can't even feed myself, and as I am pondering what the next step could be, I look up and there is José Sanchez, calling me by name and reaching for my hand."

The 53 centavos as a gambling stake had grown into many thousands of pesos via the dice and the cards. As an amputee, José had been imprisoned in Bilibid after the Bataan surrender. Since he had managed to conceal his money, he bribed the Japanese guards and paid the prisoners who went out on work details to procure for him almost anything he wanted. He even hired a prisoner to help him get around. Later José fashioned a solid wooden peg leg, and he could get around with some ease.

Ken was placed in the former execution chamber on the raised concrete platform that had been the base for the electric chair. On the wall above him was a huge painted hand and the word DANGER. Sanchez knelt and reassured him that everything was going to be all right.

Ken asked him, "Why is everything going to be all right?"

"Because I'm going to send a man to care for you each morning and each afternoon until you can take care of yourself."

Every morning an American prisoner brought a canteen of water and a rag and washed him, combed his hair, and fed him rice and a poached egg or some Filipino tidbit. At noon he received the regular camp fare, and in the evening José sent a bowl of Spanish rice, with sometimes even a small piece of meat in it. In six or seven weeks Ken was well enough to walk the length of the building, some 30 or 40 feet between the cots of the other prisoners.

Next morning José came in after breakfast and said, "Porwoll, I hear you have recovered."

"I have walked the length of this building."

"That is fine," said José. "You are recovered, and my man will no longer come to help you."

"That's all right with me," Ken said. "But tell me, José, why did you send him in the first place?"

After looking at him for some time with his sad, brown eyes, José said, "Sergeant, when I was thirsty, you gave me something to drink."

"What did I give you to drink?"

Again a long look from the sad eyes: "Beer."

Ken remembered the supplies of beer he had taken to the hot guard-house in which José had spent 30 sweltering days and nights.

After another eight weeks Ken was shipped back to Cabanatuan. Wherever he ran into men from the 194th Tank Battalion he heard similar tales of José caring for the sick in Bilibid. For anyone who was in relatively good health and wanted something extra, however, José required an IOU payable in the United States after the war, and he lived to collect.

An Associated Press report in 1959 is the last any of us has heard of José Sanchez:

Wooden Leg of Vet Put in Museum

Washington—A battered, hand-carved wooden leg once the property of a former G.I. hero of a Japanese prisoner-of-war camp in Manila, now lies in the Armed Forces Medical Museum.

The wooden leg belonged to the former Private First Class José Sanchez, whose present whereabouts are unknown. He once lived in Los Angeles.

Joseph L. Adeski, former medical-service officer, turned the leg over to the museum. He explained the soldier gave the leg to him in a hospital after World War II in exchange for a good one.

The leg is the first wooden anatomical specimen in the museum.

35

FARM DAYS

*H*UNGER WAS OUR constant companion, so much so that we rarely thought of sex. One day, perhaps to taunt us for our lack of women, the guards tied a female department-store mannequin to one side of the entrance gate. One horyo said, "I wonder how much milk she would give?"

Occasionally, dogs strayed into the camp, and once we saw a dog carrying a human forearm scavenged from the graveyard. Usually, a dog ended up in some kitchen's stew pot. Work details outside camp sometimes caught dogs. One prisoner, startled by a dog barking at him, shouted, "Woof to you, you son of a bitch," and grabbed the animal by the jaws to add to our stew.

On Christmas, the day after the Mass of the Blue Moon, Father Buttenbruch brought small packages for all 4,000 prisoners. My gift was wrapped and tied with a ribbon: razor blades, hard candies, a small tube of toothpaste, and three cigarettes. The packages had been prepared in Manila by the Masonic orders, Protestant church groups, and Catholic sodalities for young women. Also on Christmas Day the Japanese released enough Red Cross food that every prisoner was full when he slept that night.

The Red Cross sent bulk packages of sugar, powdered milk, thick beef stew, and cornmeal, and each prisoner received a 12-pound box once every three or four months during most of 1943 and early 1944. From December 1942 to March 1944 the health of the camp gradually improved. We were receiving a barely adequate diet. But as the Japanese began to be driven back, as their shipping was disrupted by American bombing and submarine attacks, the food at Cabanatuan dropped off to what it had been in 1942.

By early 1943 our morale was bolstered by reports of American advances in the South and Central Pacific. Somewhere in camp was a radio. We were careful not to know where it was, as the information might be squeezed out of us by the Japanese guards. I thought it must have been in the Japanese compound, where some prisoners worked regularly and where power would have been accessible. Through this radio and through the underground—mainly the truck drivers—we learned how the war was going and where the Americans and Australians had landed in their progress north.

Premier Hideki Tojo issued a directive that prisoners were to grow at least some of their own food, just as Japanese troops, wherever they were stationed during the war, worked on vegetable gardens. By the end of 1943 the original small farm south of the prison was expanded to 500 acres. We cultivated that land almost entirely by hand, with mattocks, picks, shovels, hoes, and rakes. Because these tools had been designed for shorter men, we found that working with them was backbreaking.

Some plowing was done with carabao, the patient, all-purpose water buffalo of the Far East. But the wooden plows were designed for the mud of a rice paddy and could not be used on the rest of the farm, particularly in the dry season when the crust of volcanic ash became cinder dry. And the carabao is slow. Having no sweat glands, the carabao needs to amble to a mud wallow now and then. One farm guard, whom we called Air Raid, went berserk with anger at a carabao that wanted time off to wallow. He grabbed the rein from the plowman and pulled the carabao around by his nose ring. The carabao lumbered into a gallop and carried Air Raid and the plow into the wallow. Air Raid, purple with anger, stood up to his waist in mud and screamed. Cooler guards prevented him from butchering the carabao. Soon the carabao was plowing again, and Air Raid was beating *us* again.

Work on the farm brought prisoners and guards into close contact. Previously, the Japanese had rarely entered the work area or the hospital area. They guarded the perimeter of the compound, manned the guard towers with rifles and submachine guns, and checked work details and hospital visitors through the gate. Now the farm detail was so large that it required many guards, and the cumbersome communication led to frequent misunderstandings.

"Dame, dame, bakayaro," the guard yells at the prisoner.

"You bastardly son of a bitch," says the prisoner, nodding pleasantly to the guard.

One day Sergeant Waterman and I were planting camotes by hand.

The guard we called Donald Duck hurried over to us, swinging his vitamin stick and shouting orders in Japanese. He made gestures and repeatedly put his head down. We didn't know what to do. Finally Waterman knelt down and stood on his head. Donald Duck looked dumbfounded, gave up, and stalked away: "America crazy, America all crazy." We later learned that we had been planting the camotes upside-down.

More often a misunderstanding had brutal results. A friend, Corporal Dwyer, spent most of an afternoon with his hands tied and pulled down over his knees and with a hoe handle thrust through under his knees and over his arms. He never knew what he had done or not done. Another prisoner, dazed from malarial fever, was being slapped and harangued by Smiley, one of the farm overseers. An American major stepped in between them and tried to reason with Smiley. Immediately, five guards trotted over and pounded the major with rifle butts. He was soon unconscious on the ground under the sickening thud of those rifle butts.

Navy Lieutenant Commander Jordan, an able speaker of Japanese, went from group to group to iron out problems and reduce the beatings. After several beatings resulted in the deaths of prisoners, Lieutenant Colonel Curtis Beecher, who had arrived from another prison camp and become the American camp commander, worked out an arrangement with the Japanese: the armed guards were posted on the perimeter of the farm, and prisoner-overseers directed the work.

At one point Air Raid decided to be a mounted overseer. He ordered Sergeant John Austin, who had fought at Argonne in the First World War and with the 31st Infantry in Bataan, to make him a saddle and bridle. Air Raid commandeered a horse from a Filipino family. When the horse, little larger than a calesa pony, had been saddled and bridled, Air Raid inspected Sergeant Austin's work and mounted. Someone had placed a Philippine thistle plant under the saddle blanket. When Air Raid swung into the saddle, the horse squealed and bucked. Air Raid went overboard. No one even looked. The laughter that might have been fatal was stored until later. Air Raid gave up his notion of being a mounted overseer.

We often saw the Japanese trainees being drilled in the garrison area and receiving punishment. The nose tweak was regarded as a more severe punishment than slaps, which were more serious than a kick. The Japanese noncommissioned officers who did this training inflicted group punishments to cure individual errors, expecting a soldier to be further disciplined by his fellow soldiers.

We also received this treatment. As a common punishment we were lined up in a double file facing one another and ordered to slap the prisoner opposite. If the slaps were not hard enough, further punishment followed. On the farm the tallest Americans were given the most frequent beatings. Lieutenant Wells Hodson, an All-American track star at the University of Minnesota, had a tremendous physique. With his lips puffed up or with a black eye, he would say, "Fitz, they certainly gave me a socking today. Didn't they get you?"

But at other times they did get me. One day I was assigned with three fellow war prisoners to clean up around the Japanese guard house. I was appointed to be in charge. We had been working for about an hour when one of the guards yelled "Kura! Baka!" and rushed at me as I bent over pulling some weeds. As I straightened up, he began to really slap me around. My ears rang for days. After about ten minutes—I stood at attention the entire time—the guard stopped and motioned to me to sit down on a nearby bench. He then joined me, reaching into his shirt pocket and pulling out a cigarette pack. He had one cigarette left which he broke into two parts, giving me half. We lit up together, though I wasn't a smoker. I never did find out why he punished me.

The American officer in charge of supplying able men for the farm work was Dr. Emil Reed, nicknamed Death Rattle Reed or Rigor Mortis Reed. Yet he was admired and liked: someone had to select the workers—and better Dr. Reed than one of the Japanese. Some of the men chosen by Dr. Reed seemed on the verge of collapse. The chaplains often worked on the farm in place of ill prisoners.

Some reports have claimed that the Japanese sold off our entire farm produce to Filipino markets. Actually, they ate one-third and sold about one-third. On the detail that distributed food to the kitchens, I saw that much of the remainder of our produce went to the prisoners.

We also grew personal gardens, carefully nurturing seeds and shoots we smuggled into camp from the farm. Sometimes hungry prisoners harvested others' crops at night, but such stealing was rare. When they were shipped out, prisoners gave their gardens to their friends left in the camp.

36
MAJOR SMOTHERS AND THE SMOTHERS BROTHERS

I N 1966 MY OLD FRIEND Harold "Snuffy" Kurvers stopped in at my insurance office with news that the Smothers Brothers would be performing as part of the St. Paul Winter Carnival. In prison camp Snuffy and I had known their father, Major Thomas Bolyn Smothers, Jr. Major Smothers died on a Japanese prison ship bombed by American planes. In 1966 I had never heard of the Smothers Brothers. My three teenaged sons shook their heads in disbelief. Since returning to civilian life, I had married and had fathered a family. I didn't have time for television, because in the evenings I was usually meeting with clients.

But I remembered Major Smothers very distinctly and had a profound respect for him. At Cabanatuan Prison Camp I had worked under him distributing food. For this job, only officers of the utmost integrity and honesty were chosen by their American superiors. Working with Major Smothers was his close friend Lieutenant Colonel Harold K. Johnson, who by 1966 had become commanding general of the U.S. Army.

I thought that Major Smothers's sons might be interested in my memories of him. They were small boys when the Second World War began—Tom was four and Dick was two—so they would hardly remember their father. I called two friends on the Winter Carnival organizing committee, Hubert "Bill" White and Henri Foussard, and asked them to ask the Smothers Brothers if they'd like to hear of their father. Word came back that the Smothers Brothers would meet me, but they were skeptical because over the years many former war prisoners had falsely claimed to have known their father. My friends had assured them, however, that if I said I knew their father, I did know him.

Bernard FitzPatrick at a memorial in the American Cemetery, near Manila, April 1967, pointing out the name of a friend and fellow war prisoner, Major Thomas Bolyn Smothers, Jr., the father of Tom and Dick Smothers. Major Smothers died on a Japanese prison ship.

To familiarize myself with their comedy, I bought a couple of their record albums at a music store, and two days later I drove out to North Oaks Country Club, where they were appearing at a Winter Carnival luncheon. We met in a back room where they were waiting to entertain the luncheon. They were wary of me at first but warmed up when they realized I really could tell them about their father.

A West Point graduate, Major Smothers was 5'8" tall and weighed 150 pounds. He had sandy hair and looked very much like his son Tom. He was rugged and well muscled, and his stride of authority was accentuated by a bamboo walking stick. Before the surrender of Bataan he was the executive officer of a crack regiment, the 45th Philippine Scouts. Only officers with considerable combat ability became executive officers.

Major Smothers was a great lover of music. In the evening after work detail he often sat on a small box chair and listened to the glee club practice. As a ranking American officer, he was very helpful in support of our glee club. Although he didn't sing with us, he loved light opera, especially Gilbert and Sullivan. The French marching song "Madelon" was one of his favorites. I sang it for his sons.

Dick asked about their father's interest in baseball because he had been quite a player at West Point. I responded that Major Smothers had played baseball in prison camp, but the field was so small and bumpy that even running was difficult. Tom asked if their father had had a nickname in prison camp. "We heard that at West Point he was called Smo," he said. I told them that Major Smothers's fellow officers called him Smo—but not an enlisted man like me.

I came to know Major Smothers well because of the nature of the ration detail. With other enlisted men accompanied by Major Smothers, I helped pick up the food from the Japanese. We would load the rice and vegetables into a carryall, similar to a stretcher borne by two men, and deliver the food to the camp's mess halls. Often the food was delayed, and we stood around chatting. I usually did not discuss military policy with officers, but I felt comfortable enough with Major Smothers to ask him what he thought of the American military strategy in the Philippines. He said, "You know, Fitz, if it weren't such a tragedy, it would be a comedy of errors."

My visit with Tom and Dick Smothers lasted about an hour and a half. I rode with them in the limousine as they made stops at various Winter Carnival events during that afternoon, and I accompanied them to the airport when they left. A year later I met them again at the Minnesota State Fair, when they performed at the main grandstand. They gave my family front-row seats, and we visited Tom and Dick backstage afterward.

Tom told me that soon after the war he and his mother and Dick traveled to San Francisco to meet a hospital ship. Their mother had been notified that Major Smothers was on board, but they found that a mistake had been made: a Major Smathers, not Major Smothers, was on the ship. It was another scene of the tragic comedy of errors.

37

SHIPPING OUT

I N THE LAST MONTHS of 1943 the Japanese ordered us to help construct an airfield. Our American camp commander, Colonel Beecher, protested, but he was ignored. The Cabanatuan airfield detail had, however, one rewarding feature. Large ants built enormous ant-hills, eight feet in diameter at the base and six feet tall. Every prisoner tried to be assigned to the group that tore down the anthills. In the cool sand of the bases of the anthills lived cobras, sometimes twelve feet long. One prisoner held a long stick rigged with a noose of wire at one end. He baited the snake into striking and snared it in the noose. The others grabbed the snake, and it was soon cut up for stew in the kitchen of the lucky prisoners. Later, when food was scarcer, the Japanese guards sometimes insisted on a share of cobra.

By then our entertainment was in full swing, thanks to Colonel Wilson's supervision during the two years that I was at Cabanatuan. Lieutenant Harvard Al Manning organized a small theater group, for which he wrote plays and acted. Without any printed texts, this group reconstructed plays from memory, sewed costumes, and built rough sets. I remember a warm performance of Dickens's *A Christmas Carol* and some hilarious acting by the British Lieutenant Sevann in Brandon Thomas's *Charlie's Aunt*.

Johnny Kratz got together a lively orchestra. Some instruments were smuggled into camp, and the Japanese allowed us to bring in a small piano from Manila. Pappy Harris still had his guitar, and soon they added a good cornet player and a drummer who made a set of drums from carabao hide. They played jazz and light classical music.

The glee club gave many concerts. We developed a repertoire of songs from all lands from Wagner's "Soldier's Chorus" to Sibelius's "Song of Peace." As more men recovered their health, we gained excellent replacement voices. Of all the songs, the most expressive of prison-camp life was "Gentlemen Rankers," an old British army song made famous by the Yale glee club as "The Whiffenpoof Song." Lieutenant John M. Wright, Jr., sang the solo part, and he seemed to sing for all of us:

> We have done with hope and honor;
> We are lost to love and truth;
> We are dropping down the ladder rung by rung.
> And the measure of our torment
> Is the measure of our youth,
> God help us, for we knew the worst too young.

On Christmas Eve 1943 we again had a midnight mass, and the new year started well. Limited supplies of Red Cross food and medicine continued to reach us. Early in 1944 almost every prisoner received shoes. To make them last as long as possible, I wore my shoes only on special occasions such as rest day, each Sunday, or when I was working with the choir or glee club. Our feet had been toughened by going barefoot, and many of us were used to wearing Japanese sandals.

In February 1944 I received my first and only mail during my time as a war prisoner. A letter from my sister Rose, a nun, was so censored and mutilated that I could make no sense of the few legible words. My only other letter was from a close friend, Dan York of St. Paul. He said that he was praying for my well-being every day and that he hoped I didn't mind if a Presbyterian prayed for me. I showed the letter to Major Maury, who laughed and said, "We're in no position to be choosy about who prays for us!" I also received a small package from my mother, sent two years earlier. There was no message—just a package with vitamin tablets, soap, a toothbrush, toothpaste, and some melted candy. I ate the candy, paper wrapper and all.

In late February the issue of food began to decrease rapidly. In March the Japanese formed medical teams of American doctors, dentists, and corpsmen and sent them to Japan. The work on the airfield near Cabanatuan was stepped up in response to the increased tempo of Allied advances. In June, Saipan fell. Prisoners from Davao were brought to Cabanatuan and put in a carefully restricted area, and prisoners were shipped to Manila, on the way to Japan. One night in early July a runner from Japanese headquarters awakened me at midnight and told me to get ready to go immediately. I had had no earlier warning.

I put what few things I had in a duffel bag. I wore my new shoes so I wouldn't lose them. Even though it was late, many of my friends, especially from the glee club and the choir, came to say goodbye. Corporal George Anderson and Sergeant Donald Nelson, excellent voices from St. Olaf College, offered to buy me a hotdog at the next St. Thomas and St. Olaf football game. Major Maury gave me a can of salmon. Major Philip Lauman asked how to find me after the war and gave me his address and 20 pesos "in case you get a chance to buy something between here and Bilibid Prison." Lieutenant Bill Tooley gave me a bar of Red Cross chocolate. Harvard Al Manning sauntered up, grinned, and said, "Next time I see you, I'll have finished my musical *Rice Pudding: The Mad Monk*. There'll be a part for you." Gus Sayre gave me some quinine, and I gave him my garden patch. I never saw any of them again. None of them survived the war.

Part Four

TO JAPAN

38

HELL SHIP

OUR TRUCKS HALTED in the town of Cabanatuan until daylight. The guards motioned us to stay in the trucks, and they leaned against the tailgate, smoking and talking in low voices. We dozed and talked. We decided that the halt was a precaution against an escape attempt in the darkness. In the soft light of dawn we saw a dog trot furtively past, and two Filipinos waved to us.

Soon we moved off toward Manila, 60 miles to the south. The going was slow. Sometimes we were held up behind lines of carabao carts, although in the towns the Japanese military police stopped traffic for us. In the barrios we would feel our truck braking, and then out of the rear of the truck we would see the chickens that had scuttled out of the way or the calesa that had edged off the road. At one of these barrios, Salangan, a group of Filipino women and children threw bananas, mangoes, and rice cakes into the truck for us. The guards paid no attention to them or to us as we divided up the food.

About noon on July 8, 1944, we reached Manila. The city was hot and muggy from the light rain. There were few people in the street, and the whole city seemed forlorn. We were unloaded, lined up, and counted by our guards. Then we were marched through the high iron gates in the 20-foot-thick concrete wall of Bilibid Prison. The gates clanged shut behind us, and we were counted off by the prison guards. We were marched to an open area in one corner and told that we were restricted to that space for the time being. We could see the fringes of the electrically charged wire strung along the tops of the walls. We were to sleep on the ground for three nights.

Bilibid Prison was laid out like a six-pointed starfish. The center held the administration and the guards, and the six arms were two-story barracks used mainly as hospital wards for the war prisoners. At each tip was a guard tower. In July 1944 Bilibid was crowded with

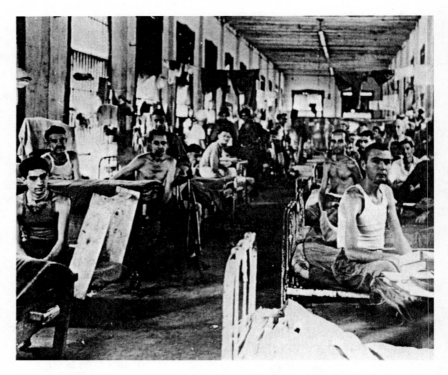

American war prisoners in a hospital in Bilibid Prison, Manila, February 1945. These American war prisoners were among the fortunate ones who were rescued by the American forces before the Japanese could ship them to Japan.

prisoners from camps all over the Philippines, awaiting shipment to Manchuria, Korea, and Japan. There were also prisoners who had skills that the Japanese required for work in Manila.

One of the prisoners already in Bilibid walked over and shook my hand. He was Jim Daly, the college friend with whom I had celebrated All Hallows in Manila. He had been seriously wounded in the heavy fighting just before the fall of Bataan. After the surrender he had been left behind in one of the field hospitals and later had been moved to Bilibid. For the past two years we had kept in touch by word-of-mouth messages conveyed by work details moving between Cabanatuan and Bilibid. Jim's left hip was still in bad shape, and he was very thin.

Jim knew the ropes of Bilibid, and he knew what was going on out in the bay on the prison ships. We talked about the taking of Tinian and Saipan by American forces and about the rumors of the imminent fall of the Tojo government. He told me that the Japanese were shocked by this news: "They seem disorganized and unsure of themselves. It becomes even more of a puzzle for them, how to deal with us. I think that's why they're speeding up on moving prisoners to Korea and Japan."

For the next two days, July 9 and 10, the Japanese kept issuing orders that our group be ready to leave, only to countermand the orders again and again. Twice while we were waiting, American prisoners were brought in from a ship and dumped back into Bilibid. Most of them came on stretchers, some dead, the rest exhausted and sick from the heat and the lack of water and food. We felt in our bones that the trip on those ships might be even worse than Cabanatuan. We knew that some unmarked prisoner-transport ships had been sunk by American forces. Jim promised to see my family if he made it through the war, and I promised I would see his family if I made it. As it happened, he got home much sooner than I did, and he visited my family because he thought I had been on a ship that was torpedoed and sunk.

On the evening of July 10 the group from Cabanatuan was alerted for departure on the following morning. Jim and I had a farewell meal together. Jim had a coconut, and José Sanchez came by and gave me, as a fellow member of the 194th Tank Battalion, some mongo beans, a generous present. Jo wished me luck and stumped off on his homemade wooden leg.

On the morning of July 11, about 1,650 of us were marched to Pier 7, the largest dock on the Manila waterfront. We waited while Filipino stevedores, under Japanese supervision, finished loading horses on a ship. Each horse was raised in a sling carefully and slowly and deposited gently on deck to be led away. Us they herded down the dock into the two holds of a nondescript Japanese freighter. The guards urged us on with gun butts and bayonets. After the war an English prisoner was asked if he had been loaded like an animal. He said, "No, we were not loaded like animals. They took good care of animals. We were loaded like coal down a coal chute."

Fourteen feet down a wide, slanting ladder, we found ourselves in a small hold with low shelves, five high along each side of the ship. Yelling guards forced us into these shelves feet first and side by side. The shelves, designed for Japanese soldiers, were too short for us by half a foot or more. Our heads hung over the edges. When all the shelves were full, the guards crammed men against the aft bulkhead of the hold. Finally, they squeezed the last man in underneath the hatch. The guards climbed out, and the crew fitted heavy planks over the opening to the hold. The crowded men on the floor could sit down only with their knees jammed under their chins. The air grew hotter and hotter. With only chinks of light visible through the planks over the hatch, the air was still, and the temperature soared.

We felt the ship moving for a short time and then heard a rumble of chain. The engines stopped. We lay at anchor out in Manila Bay for the next three days. The humidity became total as sweat oozed from everyone. Our canteens of water were soon empty. Twice a day the Japanese guards lowered buckets of rice gruel and water or weak unsweetened tea, to be shared not always fairly among far too many men. There in the heat of the hold some men lost their sanity, and we had to hold them down. Most of those men died soon afterward.

We were wracked with dysentery. Many did not have the strength to shove through the hot, slippery crowd to one of the eight five-gallon benjo cans, empty lard cans used for slop buckets. When prisoners were allowed on deck to empty the benjo cans over the side, the guards kept their distance and hosed the deck afterward. The prisoners who volunteered for this task moved as slowly as they could, to stay in the fresh air and sunlight and also to let air and light into the hold. Only when the hatch planks were removed was there enough light for us to see one another. We called the ship the *Benjo Maru*, the *Latrine Ship*, the *Toilet Tub*. During those days at anchor some prisoners died from suffocation, heat, dehydration, dysentery, malaria, or beriberi. They were hoisted roughly up on deck and were carted ashore. Some of them revived in the fresh air and were hauled back to Bilibid Prison.

On July 14 the anchor chain rumbled and clanked, and our ship began the run to Japan. Four prisoners who worked in the galley told us that there were few ships in the convoy and no escort ships. Like all the other Japanese prison ships, the *Benjo Maru* was unmarked. We knew an American submarine or carrier plane might attack us at any time. No Allied prisoner was ever issued a life preserver. The ship moved north, along the coast of Luzon, across to the west side of Formosa, and up the long chain of the Ryukyu and the Tokara islands to Kyushu and the inland sea of Japan. At sea the temperature in the hold was more bearable, cooling as we traveled north.

Early every morning a few of the planks were moved aside, and the prisoners who worked in the galley climbed the ladder. Then other

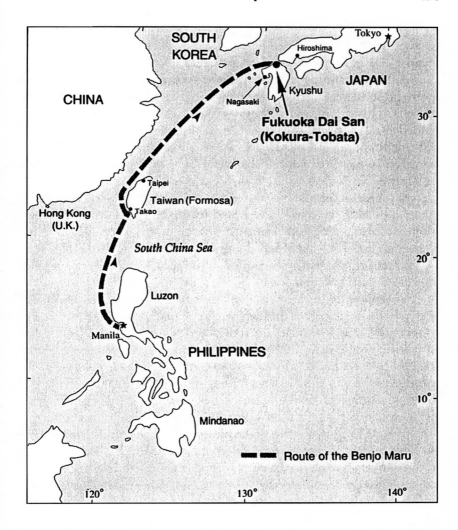

Route of the Benjo Maru, 1944. Map by Brian Kowalski and Steve Leach of the Cartography Lab of the Geography Department of the University of Minnesota.

prisoners carried up the benjo cans. Soon they lowered the empty cans and climbed down. The ship's crew replaced the planks. A little later the planks were moved again, and the galley detail lowered in buckets of lugao and water. We struggled to get our shares. I would dip my canteen cup into the water and back away to pour it carefully into my canteen. Then I would strap on the canteen so no one could take it. I would suck the last few drops of water from the canteen cup and hold it out for some of the lugao. Guarding my cup, I would move back to my place against one of the wooden shelf supports. Only then would I eat.

In the late afternoon came another lifting and lowering of benjo cans and soon afterward another lowering and lifting of water and rice buckets. The afternoon rice was better. It was dry and occasionally included a leaf of cabbage. Even this meal, as hungry as we were, became difficult to stomach by the time we reached Japan. We had to force ourselves to eat. We had to force ourselves to think it was worth going on eating.

At times we became too filthy, too stinking, and the crew removed the planks over the hatch and hosed us down with salt water. It was momentarily cooling and cleansing, but the drains were clogged. After the hatch had been battened down again, seawater, urine, and feces sloshed and rippled with the motion of the ship. Gradually, we became encrusted with salt and feces.

As the daylight through the crevices faded at night, we hoped there would be no submarine attack. A chaplain, who had volunteered to accompany us, always led us in the Lord's Prayer. Then a Jewish doctor recited Psalm 130, "De Profundis," in his clear tenor voice: "Out of the depths have I cried unto Thee, O Lord. Lord, hear my voice." We listened to the vibration of the engines and the low creaking of the hull as we pitched and rolled in the waves. Prisoners mumbled in their sleep, and sometimes a man cried out or babbled.

One evening there was an explosion, and the ship stopped. We thought we must have been bombed or torpedoed. We heard footfalls and shouting. Through the cracks between the hatch planks we saw smoke lit up by fire. Then the ship was under way again. Later one of the guards told us that a nearby ship had been torpedoed. Our ship picked up some of the Japanese crew.

On the day a close friend died, I was one of the four men to carry the litter. His naked body was covered by a blanket. We struggled up to the deck, holding the litter sideways. A chaplain, Father John Curran, followed us. We were half-blinded by the sunlight. A Japanese guard gestured to us to carry the litter to the port side. The blanket was removed. His body was so shrunken that the skin barely covered the bones. Ballast was tied to his feet. We raised the end of the litter, and his body slowly slid over the side of the ship. Father Curran prayed. The sunlight and the sea air were a refreshing shock to us, but

I felt only the loss of my friend. The prayer ended, and we were hustled below.

On the morning of August 10, 1944, the ship stopped, and the hatch was uncovered. Those of us who were still able helped those who could no longer walk. We were in Moji, Kyushu, Japan. We had been below for 30 days.

39

FUKUOKA DAI SAN

ON A LONG BOARD over the entrance, large characters in Japanese proclaimed, "Fukuoka Furyo Dai San, Kokura, Kyushu, Nippon." *Fukuoka*: prefecture or province; *Furyo*: Prison Camp; *Dai San*: Number Three; *Kokura*: the name of the nearby city, then about 200,000 in population; *Kyushu*: one of the four main islands of Japan, south of the inland sea; *Nippon*: the Japanese name for the country. The word *furyo* can also be used as a substitute for *horyo*: "bad, evil, depraved, inferior, unwholesome, wicked person."

They never oiled the gates, and the sound of opening and closing bit into our ears. The two large panels of the gates swung outward. When closed, they were barred from within by a four-by-eight beam in heavy brackets in each panel. The gates, the stockade, and the barracks reminded me of the motion-picture versions of U.S. cavalry posts in the nineteenth-century West. There was one obvious difference: no guard towers. Here the guards were on the inside with us. Obviously, we were not going anywhere. Where could one of us have hidden in Kyushu?

That first day, August 10, 1944, the guards moved us through the gates in a straggling column of fours and halted us in the main assembly area. Guards brought a table and a chair. We were about to be addressed by some official. An elderly Japanese major with unpretentious manners came to the table from a small house beside the gate. He was followed closely by an obsequious Japanese interpreter, who handed the major first onto the chair and then onto the table, and then he climbed up himself.

The camp commandant, Major Yaichi Rikitaki, was fair and just, according to Japanese standards. He paid meticulous attention to his job. He spoke in a quiet, earnest voice, gave the interpreter time to speak, and although he knew some English, as we learned later, he

Fukuoka Dai San, Kokura, Kyushu, Japan, 1944–1945.

would not use it unless he was absolutely certain his phrasing was correct.

That first afternoon Major Rikitaki gave us all the rules of the camp: we must bow to anyone in Japanese uniform, that is, stand in place with hands precisely at each side and bow, whereupon the Japanese would bow or nod to us, and we could straighten up. We must learn enough of the Japanese language to obey army commands, to count off, and to reply correctly when addressed. We could smoke only at certain times of the day. There was to be no trading with civilian workers at our place of work. No contraband was to be brought into camp. Of course, we soon found out how to circumvent the rules against trading and smuggling.

Finally, the major ordered that we be bathed and fed immediately, and he turned us over to the sergeant of the guard. We did get a bath, unbelievably welcome, though without soap for most of us. We were fed the usual evening meal of rice and vegetable soup, insufficient but far better than on the ship. Then the American medical team in camp gave us physical checkups. Dr. Anderson and most of the others had known us in Cabanatuan and were horrified at our condition after the month's voyage.

War prisoner barracks where Bernard FitzPatrick stayed at Fukuoka Dai San, 1944–1945.

The Japanese quartermaster corporal issued us work jackets, trousers made of a soft burlap cloth, low tennis shoes, and tube socks. The socks lasted for a while, but the rest quickly fell apart. Soon the G-string rags were the common uniform. The shoes rarely fit, and we learned to cut them to the shape of our feet. At last we were assigned to a barracks and given two blankets and shown the 28-inch tatami on which we were to sleep. And we slept.

For two days we rested and learned the camp routine. I met Sergeant Norman Berg, a marine who had been an embassy guard in Peking. I knew some of his relatives in Minnesota. He had been at this prison camp for more than two years. He said that life there had become more bearable since the former camp commandant had been replaced by Major Rikitaki. Norm always had positive news about the American advances in the Pacific. Such news was great for morale. So was my belief in a just God and the concept that our suffering was part of a greater plan, however incomprehensible to me. Throughout the prison-camp ordeal, many of us were sustained by a diet of rice, rumors, and religion.

On the third day those who were able went to work. I was one.

Interior of barracks where Bernard FitzPatrick stayed at Fukuoka Dai San.

We got up at 5:30 A.M., arranged our sleeping space, folded blankets, and cleaned up. At 6:00 A.M. we ate vegetable soup and dry rice, much better than the thin rice gruel at Cabanatuan. At 7:00 A.M. we fell in, counted off, and marched through the gates to the open railroad gondola cars for transporting us to work at the Yawata steel mill.

Common bath for war prisoners at Fukuoka Dai San.

As usual, we were grouped in tens. For each group, one of us served as honcho, or leader. Japanese civilian straw bosses, called pushers, assigned work to several groups at a time. Japanese military guards roved through the plant carrying rifles with bayonets ostentatiously fixed. Although they rarely understood the work, these guards were the ultimate authority there.

On the first day we did not look able: when the Japanese pusher made a fiery speech, the translation was "Don't work too hard. Keep yourselves healthy." This pusher was named Iwasaka. He was tall and swarthy, and he kept an eye open for our welfare. He warned everyone about an unusual visit from the secret police. He assigned the sick or weak prisoners to preparing the tea. He served as our go-between with the army and the civilian workers. The other pusher was Muto. He was more ordinary in appearance, gentler, and equally helpful, and he was a born trader.

Eventually we worked at many of the heavy tasks in the steel mill. We piled the bricks for lining the huge melting pots. We worked with civilian women chipping the used bricks to prepare them for reuse. We cleaned out recently used steel furnaces. We shoveled cinders into

Bernard FitzPatrick as a war prisoner at Fukuoka Dai San, 1944–1945. This photograph was taken by the Japanese.

small railroad dump cars to be hauled away and perhaps used to sur-face a prison-camp street. The Japanese civilians we worked with were old men, women, boys in their teens, veterans who had been in-capacitated in the service or were clearly faking their injuries, and a few skilled civilians who really understood the processes of steel making. We came to like and trust these people, for they were kind to us. They often shared their scanty food, and they traded with us, sometimes stealing in order to have food to trade.

Yawata Steel Works, Kokura, Kyushu, Japan 1944–1945. Allied war prisoners worked alongside Japanese women.

At first the pushers and the other civilians called me by the number on my wooden dog tag: sen roku ju roku (1066). But soon I was called Fitzu, as I had often been at the other camps. Sergeant Teramura had given me good advice back in Calauan: "Do as told and learn language." Again my professional title helped. Teacher of singing was an honored profession in Japan, and because I sang when asked to, I got along well with the civilians at work and with a good many of the camp garrison. At no time was I ever asked to say or do anything against my allegiance to the United States.

Everyone, Japanese and prisoner, took a 15-minute break in the morning and in the afternoon, when the pushers directed the honcho to brew tea. At noon we had a 45-minute break to eat and drink more tea. At the same time the guards and the civilian workers had their noon meal, but those two groups ate separately. Only the pushers could talk to each group. We got to know Iwasaka and Muto during these breaks. Both of them had been in the army and were about 50 years old, so they knew how to make the best of the system.

At 4:30 P.M. the pushers had us put our tools away. Occasionally, they allowed us to quit a few minutes earlier and wash the soot and dust from our faces and hands at a warm-water spigot. We returned by the gondola cars, and back at the stockade we were marched through the gate. An order in Japanese rang out: "Eyes left and goose step." Major Rikitaki was usually standing at his office window to acknowledge each unit with a slight bow.

The column broke up, and those whose turn it was to bathe first would make a run for the bath. For them it was a hot, refreshing luxury. When the last prisoners bathed, the water was cool and scummed over an inch thick with filth. They did not run to bathe.

After dinner tenko was held at 8:00 P.M. This was the last formation of the day. Each barracks leader called out the approach of the officer of the day and his retinue. Every prisoner had to display his wooden dog tag on its string around his neck. The barracks leader reported to the officer of the day the numbers of prisoners present, in the hospital, or absent on special duties as tailor, cobbler, kitchen help, doctor, and corpsman. Then we stood at attention and counted off in Japanese at the top of our lungs. By 9:00 P.M. the lights were out.

40

THE TRADING GAME

ALONG WITH THE CONSTANT craving for food went the craving for salt. At the Yawata steel mill we had our own method for satisfying this craving. When the large pigs of raw steel came hot from the pouring, they were stood on ends in rows. Each pig was perhaps six to eight feet long and perhaps a foot and a half square. To expedite the cooling process, the Japanese sprayed the pigs with salt water, presumably to conserve fresh water. A crust of salt built up on the pigs. Some prisoners burned their tongues by licking before the steel was cool. Usually we scraped the salt from the steel and smuggled it into camp for our rice.

My most persistent memory of Fukuoka Dai San is of the rich smell of the food cooking for the Japanese guards and the permanent camp personnel: meat, fish, rice, and, most tantalizing of all, roast duck. By American standards these soldiers were not fed luxuriously, but they were fed adequately. At Calauan, Batangas, and Candelaria we had had no envy of Captain Wakamori, Sergeant Teramura, and the other Japanese combat engineers. When they had eaten well, so had we. But here in Fukuoka Dai San the military personnel ate well, and we did not. The civilian workers in the steel mill were fed badly, but they fared better than we did. The soldiers were also issued plenty of cigarettes, but the civilians were always in short supply. And the soldiers were issued uniforms that kept them comfortably clothed, but as the war went on the civilian clothing became increasingly threadbare and patched. The decreasing availability of consumer goods—clothes, soap, cooking pots—must have eroded the spirits of the civilians.

Perhaps the bowing, the constant deference to the military, did not irritate the Japanese civilians. Like the prisoners, the most important civilian worker at the steel mill had to bow to the lowliest army private, who might return a surly nod instead of a courteous bow. The army private might have been an uneducated sharecropper a few months earlier. If the civilians were in awe of the army, they were in near terror of the Kempei Tai, the secret police. The soldiers also showed deference to the Kempei, and they could never be sure who was a member of the Kempei or an informer. When Tojo converted the Kempei, a military police force, into an omnipresent state police force, he made it subservient to the emperor alone. As the chief minister of the emperor, Tojo exercised complete control of the Kempei.

Despite the fear of the Kempei and the deference to the army, the civilians worked together in small black-market operations. They secretly traded with us, despite the stringent penalties. Because we prisoners most of all wanted food, the civilians stole it from military warehouses and ships unloading or loading. Roasted soy beans were in large supply and were easy to conceal and pass on. The prisoner could eat them on the spot or smuggle them into camp. We were issued three cigarettes a day, convenient for trade if, like me, a prisoner did not smoke. Extra canteen cups or mess kits were premium black-market items. Once in a while a vigilant prisoner could steal from the garrison clothesline. The durable military clothes could be smuggled out of camp to the steel mill and traded to a civilian, who dyed them.

Not even the clothes of Major Rikitaki were safe. Sergeant E. López of the 31st Infantry stole the major's dress pants off the line. He wore them under his prison pants and traded them at the steel works. The camp was in a turmoil when the theft was discovered. The Japanese quartermaster corporal, Nagakura, disguised himself and appeared at the steel works. Of course, his clothes were too good, and his horn-rimmed glasses were familiar. Although the civilians did not recognize him, I loudly called, "Kiotsuke," and bowed to him as was required at the approach of any military personnel. He tried to shush me up with gestures, but the warning had been given, and the would-be spy went back to camp.

Eventually, they found out that Sergeant López had stolen the pants. He was rigorously beaten and put in solitary confinement. At the next inspection, Major Rikitaki wore patched pants. We were almost sorry about the theft. We knew that with almost any camp commander other than Rikitaki, all the prisoners would have been put on zero food and hassled day and night until the pants and the thief were produced, and López would have been eviscerated.

The Japanese quartermaster corporal, Nagakura, was one of the

Crematorium where war prisoners were cremated, Fukuoka Dai San, 1944–1945.

primary links in the trading business. He was thoroughly corrupt and completely self-seeking. I don't think that he was required to keep any records. He accepted watches, cigarette holders, and pipes in exchange for clothing and tobacco, which were traded with the civilians primarily for food.

The trading became specialized. Some prisoners developed their own lines of trade and their own channels for trading. If you wished to trade a watch, you had to pass it to the prisoner whose specialty was watches. He, of course, took a small cut. He knew the best price in trade and how to avoid trouble. A prisoner who tried to cut in on that particular traffic might be pointed out secretly and be searched at the gate and sent to one of the guardhouse cages.

One of the most important means of smuggling was the sack of a G-string. Beriberi causes testicles to swell to enormous size. Prisoners who were cured never admitted it. Their G-string sacks were padded with rags on the way out of camp, and on the way back they carried roasted soy beans or coal for the heating fires. The Japanese fastidiously avoided prisoners with dysentery, beriberi, or tubercular coughs. Few G-strings were ever searched. The Japanese could see that the stoves were burning more coal and charcoal than was issued. But to notice officially would involve a loss of face in the recognition that we had outfoxed them. Our spirits lifted happily with each successful venture.

The trading game had its odd moments. From a shared Red Cross package I acquired a small round tin of shoe polish. I put the shoe polish on my blanket for inspection. It was not worth hiding and I couldn't eat it, so why not. A new sergeant of the guard, one of the rotating group from the nearby army units, picked up the tin of polish and asked about it. He replaced it on the blanket, but that evening after dark he strolled by and offered me his morning rice in return for the tin of polish. Early the next morning he met me behind the barracks and traded his rice.

Toward the end we were running out of things to trade, and the civilians had less food. Our hunger increased. In the early spring of 1945 I felt that I could not take another winter in prison camp. Other prisoners felt the same way, as though the attrition of health and spirits had finally worn down to the bone. Now when prisoners became ill, they often went very fast. My friend Corporal Bob Wheeler went to work one morning singing "Donegal." He started coughing on the way back, and he was dead the next day.

41

THE LONE RANGER

W E HAD ARRIVED at Fukuoka Dai San near Kokura, at the northern end of the island of Kyushu, in August 1944. At about that time the U.S. Army Air Corps began bombing Japan from bases in China. On August 20 they bombed the Yawata steel works, and the bombing increased in intensity until the late spring of 1945. After each raid one plane would circle around, presumably photographing the results. The Texas Rangers allegedly sent only one man to stop trouble no matter how serious, and so we nicknamed this plane the Lone Ranger. We were proud of the Lone Ranger. He was a morale booster for us because the Japanese could not knock him down.

Before August 1944 there was little shelter against air raids. A railroad tunnel through the mountainside was half a mile away, close enough to hide quickly the electric train engines, built by General Electric in the United States. But the tunnel was too far for civilian workers or prisoners. When the first air raid came, the guards and civilian overseers laughed about the air-raid sirens and said it was a test run. Then all the sirens sounded again. The guards, with fixed bayonets, herded the 300 of us out of the steel mill and into a small, corrugated-iron building that looked like a large blacksmith shop. After locking us in, the guards ran off, displaying no bushido spirit at all.

We had all been under bombardment before. We lay on our faces on the sand and cinders of the floor, and as the sticks of bombs came slowly closer, a man who had been in the air-warning system on Corregidor estimated how far away they were and what size of bombs the B-29s were dropping. The corrugated-iron building shuddered, and we stayed flat, shoulder to shoulder on the floor. He said, "They are getting closer," and then all at once he said, "Grab onto the dirt. Here they come." Two bombs from the stick straddled us. One hit near the farther door of the building, and the other hit right outside the door

The concrete command post and air-raid shelter for the camp commander, Fukuoka Dai San. During American bombing raids, Major Yaichi Rikitaki, the camp commander, would yell from his protected post that war prisoners should take cover, but there was no suitable cover to take.

we had entered. Corrugated-iron sheeting was blasted off each end of the building, but no one was hurt or even scratched.

The guards waited a long while after the last bomb before straggling back for us. We inspected both of the bomb craters, each big enough to hold a medium tank easily. We were loaded into the railroad gondola cars and taken back to Dai San.

The Japanese guards and civilians were never as confident after that. They built shelters for themselves in the Yawata steel works. The bombings by the B-29s out of China steadily increased. They became heavier as more planes based on Guam and Tinian raided Japan. The intensity of the bombing became so great that it seemed as if the planes were over us all the time. Now we were losing comrades from the bombing, as well as from starvation, disease, and lack of medical care.

After they lost Okinawa in June 1945, the Japanese prepared for an American invasion. Okinawa was only 300 miles from the Japanese mainland and was considered part of Japan. One morning in July we were transported as usual to the Yawata steel mill but were halted for

Military training of housewives with bamboo spears, Japan, 1945. Photo by Shunkichi Kikuchi.

a while because the Japanese civilian workers were using our assembly area for practice. Older men, women, and teenaged boys were thrusting sharpened bamboo sticks into suspended stuffed sacks.

I asked our pusher, old Iwasaka, "Nani ka?" ("What's going on?")

He pointed to the writing on a large blackboard near the overseers' shack and said, "We will meet the American assault troops and fight with our spears to the death."

I responded, "Nani ka?" and pointed to myself.

"Fitzu, hanashi nai." ("I'm not talking.")

I later asked the same question of Muto, our other pusher. He said that when the invasion began, all the war prisoners would be killed.

One day in early August the Lone Ranger dropped leaflets throughout Kokura and the Yawata steel works. These leaflets, in Japanese and English in accordance with the Geneva Convention, told the Japanese military to get everyone out of that area because the B-29s would return in three days and destroy it. The guards tried to collect the leaflets to prevent the civilians and prisoners from learning about this warning. But the leaflets were passed from hand to hand. The exact terms of the warning were known to everyone within a few hours.

On that third day, August 9, 1945, the Japanese marched us back into the steel mills along with the civilians, the old men and women and young boys. My job that morning was to act as honcho, straw boss of nine prisoners. Three of them were too sick to work, so I had to keep track of the six other men while the guards yelled, "Shigoto!" ("Work!") We were laboring on a brick kiln inside the steel mill.

I asked an old Japanese woman, "Hitoki aruka?" ("Are there planes up there?")

She answered, "Hai, hitoki tokusan." ("Yes, many planes.")

I gave her a cigarette, and as usual she gave me a part of her lunch. She often said she could get more at home, and we could not. Above the rumblings of the steel works, we heard a drone at another pitch. Hundreds of B-29s in the sky sounded like a tornado.

I said, "Mama san, hitoki aruka?"

She said, "Ima." ("Right now.")

Just then a Japanese guard with his rifle and bayonet came and yelled, "Shigoto!"

I yelled back, "Shigoto, my ass!" I called to my fellow prisoners, "Get out of here!"

The first sticks of bombs hit that section of the steel mill. We took cover wherever we could, while the guards ran off to their new concrete shelters and trenches.

This time firebombs were coming down in parachutes, and in a few minutes the whole countryside was on fire. The phosphorous bombs ignited the wood and paper houses, everything but the metal of the steel mills. The fire draft drew the smoke inward and up, and soon the smoke practically blotted out the sky.

The immediate thought in our minds was hunger, as usual. Maybe the guards had left their tin lunch boxes. So under the bombardment we took turns going back into the steel works to grab food. We were not brave, just gnawingly hungry. When it was Tommy Patten's turn, he dived back into the mill and was gone longer than the agreed-upon 15 minutes. So help me, I sat there and ate his food. At least 20 minutes had gone by, and I was sure he was dead. I said a prayer for him, a sort of grace. Then out of that inferno of fire and explosions came Tom with three lunch boxes and his clothes burnt off. We immediately began eating.

Suddenly he looked at me and said, "Where's my lunch?"

"Tom," I said, "I thought you were dead."

"You thieving bastard!"

Through the smoke I caught a glimpse of a plane I thought was the Lone Ranger. I said, "Tom, the Lone Ranger is up there longer than usual."

"Maybe we're more photogenic today than normal," Tom remarked.

The plane kept circling lazily, for 45 to 60 minutes, rather than for the usual 10 to 15 minutes. Then the plane flew south.

We had heard that the recent air raid at Hiroshima had involved new "super bombs." Later, in Okinawa on our way home, we learned that the final Lone Ranger had been carrying the second atomic bomb and that Kokura and the Yawata steel mill was the primary target. The bombsight specialist couldn't zero in, however, because of all the smoke from the poorly coordinated firebomb raid, so the bomber proceeded to its secondary target, Nagasaki.

A little over a month later, as the first step in our journey home, we went by train to Nagasaki to board a British aircraft carrier that would take us to Okinawa to be sorted out and flown to Manila. No one had told us about Nagasaki or the atomic radiation, and we had no repatriation personnel with us. The Nagasaki railroad station was gone. The train stopped at the end of the tracks, and we walked to the harbor over debris. The streets were hardly distinguishable from the leveled buildings. No work crews were cleaning up, and few people were around. To us Nagasaki was just another Japanese city bombed flat like Moji, from which we had just come.

For a few hours near an improvised dock we milled around like tired skeletal sheep brought to water after a drought and unwilling to leave the water and graze again. As we waited for a landing-craft tank to come and ferry us out to the carrier, Tom picked up a small rock to shy at me, and I picked one up. The rock crumbled in his hand.

"Even the rocks are going to hell, Fitzu," he said.

My rock crumbled too.

42

THE VOICE OF THE CRANE

FOR SEVERAL DAYS after the bombing on the morning of August, 9, 1945, we remained within the prison compound and occupied ourselves with the routine tasks usual to yasumi days, rest days. We cleaned the barracks. We hung out blankets to air in hopes of ridding them of bedbugs and lice. A close friend from Cabanatuan, Sergeant Carl Foster, and I cut each other's hair, according to the rules of the Japanese army. Our heads were supposed to be shaven, like the heads of the soldiers of the emperor, but razor blades were unavailable, so we used blunt scissors. We watched the guards for a clue as to what was happening. When we prodded them for further details, they muttered, "Dame, dame, baka." ("No good, so-and-so.")

On the morning of August 13 our interpreter, Warrant Officer Ed Haase, announced that 80 prisoners had been called for work. At the steel works a few civilian Japanese workers were attempting to repair the equipment damaged by the bombing. Our contingent began removing debris from the railroad spurs. There was no sense of urgency— no "Kura!" or "Shigoto!" In the late afternoon on our return to Dai San I saw the smoldering ruins of houses and other wooden structures. The devastation aroused in me neither pleasure nor sympathy.

The work groups were somewhat larger on August 14. Occasionally, I heard a distant early warning siren, but there was no air raid.

On August 15 four hundred prisoners, about half of us, returned to work at the steel mill. Some parts of the plant were in operation again. Many more of the Japanese civilian laborers and the Korean indentured laborers were back at our section of the plant. We continued to clear away debris. As usual, a guard separated the civilians from the prisoners. The small supply train, pulled by a little engine with "Düsseldorf" emblazoned on each side, was puffing through the area, but its flatcars were almost empty of scrap iron and bricks.

213

"Japan: The Peaceful Reign" (The "Kimigayo"). English translation by Sakuzo Takada.

Toward noon our guards were huddled with the civilian overseers, whom they had previously avoided. Then they rounded us up and ordered us to the gondolas. I noticed that the guards had fastened their lunch boxes to their belts, as though they would not be returning that day. We walked to the gondola cars and went through the usual routine before boarding the train. "Tenko!" ("Roll call!") "Bango!" ("Count off!") "Ichi, ni, san, shi. . . ."

Silently, the Japanese men, women, and boys crowded around a loudspeaker near us. Everyone faced toward Tokyo. Some of the Korean laborers stood at the edge of the group. There was no conversation or shuffling of feet. The big clock over the door of the overseers' shed showed a minute to noon. The steel works became silent.

A Japanese noncom yelled, "Kiotsuke!" ("Attention!") "Kei rei!" ("Bow!") But the usual next command, "Nare!" ("Recover!"), was not given. And then out of the speaker came the "Kimigayo," the Japanese national anthem, to Western ears slightly mournful, very simple, and powerful: "May thy peaceful reign last long! May it last for thousands of years, until this tiny stone will grow into a massive rock and the moss will cover it all deep and thick." Then a thin, high-pitched tone, the Voice of the Crane, descendant of Amaterasu the Goddess of the Sun, the 124th emperor, Hirohito, began to speak:

> To Our good and loyal subjects:
>
> After pondering deeply the general trends of the world and the actual conditions obtaining in Our empire today, We have decided to effect a settlement of the present situation by resorting to an extraordinary measure.
>
> We have ordered Our government to communicate to the governments of the United States, Great Britain, China, and the Soviet Union that Our empire accepts the provisions of their joint declaration.
>
> To strive for the common prosperity and happiness of all nations as well as the security and well-being of Our subjects is the solemn obligation which has been handed down by Our Imperial Ancestors and which We lay close to heart. Indeed, We declared war on America and Britain out of Our sincere desire to ensure Japan's self-preservation and the stabilization of East Asia, it being far from Our thought either to infringe upon the sovereignty of other nations or to embark upon territorial aggrandizement.
>
> But now the war has lasted for nearly four years. Despite the best that had been done by everyone—the gallant fighting of military and naval forces, the diligence and assiduity of Our servants of the state and the devoted service of Our one hundred million people—the war situation has developed not necessarily to Japan's advantage, while the general trends of the world have all turned against her interest. Moreover, the enemy has begun to employ a new and most cruel bomb, the power of which to do damage is indeed incalculable, taking the toll of many innocent lives.

Should we continue to fight, it would not only result in an ultimate collapse and obliteration of the Japanese nation, but also it would lead to the total extinction of human civilization. Such being the case, how are We to save the millions of Our subjects or to atone Ourselves before the hallowed spirits of Our Imperial Ancestors? This is the reason why We have ordered the acceptance of the provisions of the joint declaration of the powers.

We cannot but express the deepest sense of regret to our allied nations of East Asia, who have consistently cooperated with the empire toward the emancipation of East Asia. The thought of those officers and men, as well as others who have fallen in the fields of battle, those who died at their posts of duty, or those who met with untimely death and all their bereaved families, pains Our heart night and day. The welfare of the wounded and the war sufferers and of those who have lost their homes and livelihood are the objects of Our profound solicitude. The hardships and sufferings to which Our nation is to be subjected hereafter will be certainly great. We are keenly aware of the inmost feelings of all ye, Our subjects. However, it is according to the dictate of time and fate that we have resolved to pave the way for a grand peace for all generations to come by enduring the unendurable and suffering what is insufferable.

Having been able to safeguard and maintain the structure of the imperial state, We are always with ye, Our good and loyal subjects, relying upon your sincerity and integrity. Beware most strictly of any outbursts of emotion, which may engender needless complications, or any fraternal contention and strife, which may create confusion, lead ye astray, and cause ye to lose the confidence of the world. Let the entire nation continue as one family from generation to generation, ever firm in its faith of the imperishability of its divine land and mindful of its heavy burden of responsibilities and the long road before it. Unite your total strength to be devoted to the construction for the future. Cultivate the ways of rectitude; foster nobility of spirit; and work with resolution so as ye may enhance the innate glory of the imperial state and keep pace with the progress of the world.

When the speech ended, the strains of the "Kimigayo" hid the sounds of weeping. For many of them this was the first time they had heard the voice of their emperor. Overwhelmed as they were, they could hardly grasp his message.

We headed curiously toward our train, and the guards waved us aboard without counting us off, checking for contraband, using the vitamin stick or yelling "Speedo! Speedo!" The unnatural quiet was awesome.

43

YASUMI

AFTER THE EMPEROR'S noon speech on August 15, 1945, when we returned to Dai San, the guards didn't inspect us for contraband. Ed Haase, our interpreter inside the camp, announced that the remainder of the day would be yasumi, rest time. The guards neglected to make their routine stops to harass us about smoking in the barracks, gathering in groups, or visiting other barracks.

In the late afternoon the light-duty men, who were cleaning up near the high wooden fences, smuggled in some copies of the *Mainichi Shimbun*, one of the largest Japanese newspapers, with the text of the emperor's noon speech translated from his archaic court Japanese into standard written Japanese. An English translation by Ed Haase and others was soon passed from barracks to barracks. We thought we had better go on acting like prisoners. We had tenko that night, and the next day was yasumi also.

On the next day, August 16, we stayed in our barracks, resting, talking quietly, and waiting. The guards were on duty, but they never went far from the guardhouse. The daily routine was crumbling.

August 17 was another day of yasumi. In the afternoon every prisoner received a 12-pound Red Cross box of food and extra rice and vegetable stew. We found it difficult to stop eating. One prisoner immediately ate his entire Red Cross box. He had been a 200-pound marine, reduced to 109 pounds. He died that night.

During the next few days the guards stayed away from us. The prison commander, Major Rikitaki, remained in his quarters across from the guardhouse. When Sergeant Kawasaki, one of the more friendly soldiers, walked past me in front of the barracks, he merely nodded and said, "Senso owari." ("The war is over.") He did not stop to talk.

Corporal Andy Aquila, whom I'd known since Clark Field, slapped me on the back and exclaimed, "Fitz, we made it." I looked at him. He looked at me. We were skin and bones.

On August 19 Major Rikitaki told one of our senior officers that American planes would drop food and other supplies the next day. August 20, 1945, was a great relief. Around noon the B-29s began parachuting food, medicine, clothing, and tobacco in 50-gallon drums. We cheered as white chutes, red chutes, and blue chutes popped open in the air and swayed down just outside the prison area. Two chutes didn't open. One killed a Japanese civilian, and one hit a blanket and drove two feet into the hard ground, bursting and scattering canned provisions. The British soldier who had been sitting on the blanket a few moments earlier came back from the benjo, picked up his book, and looked at me over his horn-rimmed glasses. "Fitzu," he said, "I see that one of your chain stores has been through today." And he went back to reading.

The dark, metal drums and their chutes were collected by a group appointed by the British senior officer, Major D. P. Stokes, and Father Curran and Dr. Anderson, two of the most energetic and trusted Americans. This group took the drums to a supply building and set up a guard to issue equal portions of food to every prisoner, regardless of country or rank.

Some prisoners acted drunk with the sudden food. They scraped up the fruit and meat from smashed cans, along with dirt and sand, and anointed their hair, faces, and starved bodies, like cats rolling in catnip. Eating the food was like a needle jolt of stimulant. The prisoners called this euphoria a food jag. Dr. Anderson warned us that our bodies would take time to become used to these foods after the years of slow starvation. For some prisoners the new food acted like a laxative but did not impair their pleasure of eating.

The B-29s came every other day with food, medicine, clothing, insecticides, shaving equipment, tobacco, pipes, and cigarettes. On August 26 the flow of provisions was interrupted by a typhoon. We sat in the barracks, eating, talking, smoking, sleeping, and eating again. The flexible barracks, of unpainted wood joined with pegs of the same wood rather than nails, could lean at a sharp angle in the violent storm without crashing down on our heads.

Eventually, I ran over to visit Dr. Jerry Greenspaun, the leader at the next barracks. He had been one of the medical detachment who had come from Cabanatuan to Fukuoka Dai San in the spring of 1944,

Left: Captain Thomas R. Taggart, war-prisoner dentist, Fukuoka Dai San, at the war's end, August 1945. Captain Taggart retired as a colonel. *Right:* American, Dutch, and British flags made from parachutes by Corporal Clarence Houskie, Fukuoka Dai San, September 1945.

and we had been glad to meet again. Dr. Greenspaun was lying on his tatami in his small room when I knocked and put my head in. He nodded imperturbably when I asked if I could come in and talk awhile. I sat cross-legged on the tatami next to him and told him that for several days I had had the eerie feeling that I would not be able to make the change to nonprisoner life. He said it was a natural feeling. We drank saki and talked for a while, and he said, "How about singing 'The Gypsy Love Song'?" I sang it and began to feel less tense. I went out of the back door into the high winds of the typhoon and back to my barracks and a long, deep sleep until morning. By the next day the typhoon had blown itself out.

Despite the lack of surveillance by the guards and although the gate was open, we rarely left camp in those early days of yasumi. Details foraged for fresh vegetables and charcoal. In the rice kitchens, in the sand pits used for heating in the winter, and outside on the bare ground, men were continually cooking snacks. Often they made crazy combinations. We had all sworn that as soon as the war was over we would tear down the huge, flimsy wooden fences around the camp, and a couple of British soldiers and I kicked out some boards to burn for cooking. But then we stopped. No one kicked out another board. "It wouldn't look right with no fence," said a horyo.

On the morning of August 28 the B-29 drops resumed. Corporal Clarence Houskie cut up three of the multicolored parachutes. He was a lantern-jawed coal miner from Pennsylvania, and he had been a machine gunner for the toughest of outfits, the 31st Infantry Regiment. Now his huge hands operated a tiny Japanese sewing machine to make three full-size flags—American, British, and Dutch—all in the colors of the parachutes: red, white, and blue.

44

MAJOR RIKITAKI SURRENDERS

WHEN WE WOKE on the morning of September 2, all the guards had gone. Only Major Rikitaki remained. Quite early he came out of his quarters across from the guardhouse and asked Ed Haase to ask Major Dorris, the senior American officer, to assemble all the men in camp. Major Rikitaki was an older man who had been called back into the army as a reservist. For this occasion he had put on his best uniform.

When we had all gathered, he told us that the war was over. The surrender had been signed on the battleship *Missouri* in Tokyo Bay. He unstrapped his samurai sword and offered it to Major Dorris, who hardly knew what to do with it. Major Rikitaki said that he had ordered the garrison to leave their side arms and rifles in the guardhouse. From now on we would be on our own. He thanked us for obeying his rules. He saluted and walked away through the gate.

That day a small formation of navy Hellcats came roaring in, and each plane did a tight roll overhead to signify the surrender on the *Missouri*. But we did not recognize the "victory roll."

The Allied officers, Major Dorris, Major Stokes of the Royal Air Force, and Father John Curran, the highest-ranking chaplain, formed a guard company from all the national groups in Dai San. With rifles and ammunition, we could protect ourselves against any out-of-control Japanese soldiers roaming the smashed towns and countryside of Kyushu. Because the Japanese had expected this island to be the first point of the invasion, many army units were stationed near us. In the nearby city of Fukuoka, close to a major army base, the garrison assembled the American prisoners, who were mostly pilots, tied their hands behind their backs, forced them to kneel, and ceremonially beheaded them. They took photographs of this procedure. Then the executioners committed hara-kiri.

221

When Corporal Houskie's three flags were raised on flagpoles, each group sang its national anthem. It was very satisfying to us as a way of discarding our horyo status. By coincidence the radio rebuilders were twiddling dials just as the last of the national anthems died away. We heard the squeal of static, and then one of the rebuilders yelled, "Hold everything, you horyo!"

A voice came through loud and clear: "This is the United States of America, your armed-forces radio station, San Francisco, California. We will conclude this broadcast with Bing Crosby and chorus singing 'White Christmas.'" This was our first radio contact with America since the surrender on Bataan. When the song ended, we moped around and stared into space. Whenever I hear that song now it presses some invisible nerve for that moment on Kyushu.

A few days after our flag raising, an American navy medical team arrived in Dai San. They checked all of us and then escorted to a hospital ship the most seriously ill men—those with beriberi or tuberculosis, those who were blind or deaf from malnutrition, and those who had lost legs.

We must have looked strange to the first healthy Americans who saw us. We looked strange to ourselves. Our faces were swollen, and our stomachs bulged unevenly. Our flesh was soft, as though water had collected under the skin, and the skin broke easily when scraped. An army repatriation team identified us, counted us, weighed us, and arranged transportation for us. Both the navy medical team and the army repatriation team asked us to wait until we could be repatriated in large groups or as a whole. We were satisfied by this arrangement because we had just about everything we had dreamt of. We had clean clothes, good shoes, tobacco, and lots of nutritious food.

On a fine morning, soon after the army repatriation team had gone, a spotless, chauffeur-driven limousine pulled in through the gates of Dai San. Sergeant Gerry Foley stepped out of the back seat. Gerry and I had seen many days together since our first training at Fort Lewis, Washington, back in April 1941. Now he insisted that I stay with him in Moji. "It's going to be days, a week at least, before they get you guys out of here. Come on down to Moji and yasumi in luxury with Dai Ichi" ("Number One"). He hauled me off in that fancy car.

In the short distance from Kokura to Moji the chauffeur drove slowly to avoid the rubble and huge holes in the streets. Moji had been a major port of perhaps 400,000 people, but a massive bombing raid early that summer had reduced it to rubble, and there had been more raids later.

Gerry and I had come from the Philippines on the same prison ship. He'd been kept in Moji to work as a stevedore for several months, but then he acquired a special detail. On a summer job with the California forestry service during his college days, Gerry had learned how to set dynamite charges to blast out rock. In the early fall of 1944 when the bombing raids on Kyushu became frequent and serious, he headed a crew that made bomb shelters by blasting tunnels in the high, steep hills around Moji, first for the mayor and other civilian officials and then for the most important brothel madam and the rich families of Moji.

He had been allowed to pick his own crew, and as the bombing increased, he and his crew ate better than most prisoners and received medicine and medical attention. By padding his crew with men who were in bad shape, he could provide them with better food and medical care. A friend of mine, Bill Kinler, says that Gerry Foley saved his life by putting him on the blasting detail. Eventually, Gerry became the unofficial American Dai Ichi.

Gerry and a couple of his friends took me up to the air-raid shelter that he and his crew had blasted out for themselves. You had to bend over to enter, but the tunnel ran 50 feet into the mountainside and was about 8 feet wide. They had partially timbered it like a mine shaft and had carpeted it with thick, rough tatami. They still had some reserve food, mainly pickled fish. Their only danger had been a direct hit at the entrance or a landslide sealing them in.

In Moji, Gerry had appropriated one of the few undamaged houses. Two Japanese boys kept house and cooked on the charcoal braziers. The crew members living there were British corpsmen from a medical detachment, a Canadian, and an Aussie. Pappy Harris, whom I remembered well from Cabanatuan, played a small organ in the house. We all settled down to sing and eat and drink. They had enjoyed the full benefit of the B-29 drops.

The last night I spent with Gerry we went to a bombed-out part of Moji. We picked our way through the rubble to a makeshift gate and into a shabby but intact building. Gerry introduced me to the town's leading madam, for whom he had built one of the shelter caves. She seated us at a low table with beer, saki, and delicacies such as rice cookies and bits of fresh fish. Gerry asked her to talk about her large prewar business in Shanghai, where she had learned English, partly from the American marines there. All of a sudden a small boy, in an American cowboy outfit complete with two toy six-guns, came trotting into the room. He flashed his guns and said, "Bang, bang!" He was a grandson of the madam. There in the ruined city, with the saki flowing, with geishas playing their tinkling music, civilian businessmen and Japanese officers wore their samurai swords and side arms, and the recent horyo, also carrying side arms, received a red-carpet welcome.

After three days I returned to my barracks in Gerry's limousine. The B-29 food drops were continuing. Then we received the news that on Sunday, September 16, we would leave Dai San forever.

45

PÈRE RENÉ ROULLIER

I N THE WARM, misty afternoon sunshine of Thursday, September 13, 1945, most of the Allied prisoners were relaxing in front of their barracks. The barracks were so infested with lice, bedbugs, fleas, and rats that we lived outside unless rain forced us inside. The B-29s dropped more food, medicine, soap, tobacco, and clothes. The clothes flopped about our shrunken bodies, but they were clean and warm and free of vermin. As I sat in front of my barracks wondering about leaving on the next Sunday, a British officer, F. John Blake of the Royal Air Force, came through the gates.

As soon as the camp had come under our control, some of the British officers produced hidden swagger sticks and went on long walks. We Americans were amused by the pipe-in-mouth, baton-in-hand pairs of British officers on their constitutionals. Jack Blake and Major Stokes never paraded their rank or carried swagger sticks, but Jack had a pipe and, despite his dysentery, he hiked about the countryside. He was tall and fair, and he always looked spruce and cheerful, despite his drawn face and emaciated body. He had been taken prisoner at the fall of Singapore in February 1942. His father had been in the import-export business in Belgium, and Jack had grown up in Liège, but he had been educated at Oxford. He spoke several languages fluently, including Japanese.

He sat down with me on my folded blanket and described the beautiful countryside out beyond the town and the steel works. The trees were bright with fall colors all through the low mountains, and the valleys were full of families harvesting their small plots of land.

Jack had seen a man kneeling under a small pine tree. Because the man had a flowing beard, Jack had guessed he was a westerner. The man was very thin, and yet his face seemed tranquil. Jack greeted him in Japanese, and the man replied in oddly accented Japanese. Jack then spoke to him in French. The bearded face lit up, and the man began talking as though starved to speak his native language. He was a French priest named Père René Roullier, the pastor of a small parish church in the nearby city of Tobata. He had recently been released from a civilian concentration camp, where he had been interned after the fall of Germany. He said that when Jack had seen him kneeling under the pine tree, he had been praying for something to eat. After Jack told several other British and American soldiers about Father Roullier, we gathered a large sack of food, and early Friday morning Jack went off to Tobata to deliver this gift.

That evening Major Stokes, in full uniform, came to our barracks. "Fitz, old boy," he said, "would you mind leading our contingent in some farewell songs?" I felt complimented, since the British were usually aloof. At his barracks we sang "The Jolly Coachman," "Kiss Me Good Night, Sergeant Major," "Men of Harlech," "Long Way to Tipperary," and others. Then Major Stokes conferred with Sergeant Major Ales, who called everyone to attention and announced that I would lead them in "God Save the King." I'm sure my Irish ancestors turned over in their graves. We shook hands and wished one another well. After the war I corresponded with Major Stokes for years.

Early Saturday evening Jack and I walked to Father Roullier's house. Since I did not smoke, I took along a pipe and my allotment of pipe tobacco from the B-29 parachute drops. Father Roullier greeted us with a Japanese bow and said, "Komban wa." ("Good evening.") He led us into his austerely furnished house. He showed us his tiny garden and introduced us to a Japanese woman, Niki Ikeda, who served as his catechist and played the little organ in the church. She brought hot cups of sugared coffee made from the supplies that Jack had delivered the day before. Father Roullier spoke no English, and my French was too rusty for me to catch the machine-gun bursts of language that he and Jack exchanged. But Jack translated and shot my remarks off to Father Roullier so that I wasn't left out of their conversation.

Father Roullier and his parishioners had built the small church and a school building, both of which the military had commandeered in the final months of the war. They had torn down the school, but they recently had returned the church to him. His years in Japan had made him ambivalent about the war. He loved his Japanese parishioners and he hated the war. Some of his favorite students had served in the war, and he loved them no less. The Japanese constitution recog-

Père René Roullier with sisters Nami (far left) and Niki Ikeda (third from the right) and some friends at their school in Tobata, Kyushu, Japan, 1950.

nized four religions: Shinto, Buddhism, Protestantism, and Roman Catholicism. This tolerance was fairly universal throughout Japan, partly because all the Japanese paid their respects to the State Shinto, the ceremonial national reverence distinct from the Shinto religion. The people of Tobata had been kind to Father Roullier. The priest at an Episcopal church in the mountains near Tobata had died during the war, and Father Roullier's parish had cared for the priest's widow and had taken food to the people of that church.

When Father Roullier asked Jack what we had done to pass the time after work in the steel mill, Jack mentioned that I had often led the camp in singing. Father Roullier asked me if I knew any songs in French. The old French army song "Madelon" came immediately to mind, and I sang, "Quand Madelon vient nous servire à boire." Father Roullier sang with me, and his face brightened with memories of his youth in the French army.

At 10:00 P.M. we began to leave, as we knew that Father Roullier had to get up early and hear confessions before mass. Father Roullier asked if we would return the next morning and join him and the parish in the offering of the mass. He said that the militarists, backed by the

State Shinto, were already laying groundwork to discredit the American occupation forces. Father Roullier believed that a mass attended by Allied servicemen, especially Americans, would help counter this propaganda, which might persuade people suffering the shock of defeat. We assured Father Roullier that we would bring as many others as we could. He looked a little alarmed at that: "Mais c'est une petite église." We promised not to bring the whole camp. He walked us to the doorstep and bowed: "Sayonara tomadachi." ("Goodbye friends.")

As we entered through the gates of the stockade, we felt more secure. Before we turned in, Jack and I explained Father Roullier's request to some of our friends, and they passed the word along.

46

SAYONARA

ALMOST THE WHOLE CAMP was up early the next morning, in anticipation of leaving Dai San that afternoon. Quite a group assembled with Jack and me. We ate breakfast together, a delicious mixture of Spam, the new C rations, and canned fruit, all flavored with salt and some garlic.

As we walked toward Father Roullier's church, I looked around at my companions. Near me was Chin Li, who had fought with the Allies at Singapore. Jacques Poublon of Java, barely recovered from beriberi, was speaking French with Jack Blake. Jock Eastern from Edinburgh smoked his pipe and listened to three Australians and two Canadians argue about rugby. The Aussies claimed that Australian rules made for a better game, and the Canadians insisted that Australian rules meant no rules at all. Royal Dutch soldiers, White Russians, Pakistani, men from India, and several Americans—Catholic, Protestant, and Buddhist, we all went most gladly to church that Sunday. I walked first with one group and then another to find out who could follow the Latin hymnal and who could hold a tune.

When we entered the gray, unpainted church, we found people already sitting on mats facing the altar. Near the back of the church Niki Ikeda was at the organ. She stood as I walked over to her.

We bowed, and I said, "O hayo musume san." ("Good morning, Miss Young Lady.")

She said, "O hayo heitai san." ("Good morning, Mr. Soldier.")

I brought the singers to the organ and asked Niki what she and the congregation would like to sing. She suggested "Panis Angelicus," one of my favorite hymns, and she handed us copies of the St. Gregory hymnal, the hymnal I had used all my life. For a moment my hands shook. The atmosphere in the church was extremely quiet and tense.

Father Roullier approached the altar and bowed. At his side knelt

229

Paul and Joseph, who had trained as kamikaze pilots and now served as apprentice priests and lived with Father Roullier. Father Roullier prayed. Niki played the introduction to "Panis Angelicus," and we sang in Latin. Softly, the members of the parish joined us. Later we sang hymns in Latin and Japanese. The tension diminished, and people no longer sat rigid. At the end of the mass we sang "The Ave of Lourdes" in French.

We slowly left the church. The parishioners quietly gathered to greet us, and the mayor of Tobata shook hands with me. He said, "Tomadachi." Father Roullier shepherded us down the street to the large house of a Japanese couple who were parishioners. They bowed to each of us and murmured, "O hayo tomadachi" and "O hayo heitai san," as we took off our stiff new shoes before entering. They sat on mats, but they provided cushions for Jack and me.

The gathering was awkward, but the house was soon full of multilingual conversation. French, Japanese, and English, with phrases in Dutch, Hindi, and Russian, poured out of us. Everyone smiled and occasionally bowed and sipped the green tea. I accepted a cigarette that someone offered. I didn't smoke, but it would have been impolite to refuse such a scarce gift.

The time was slipping away, and I asked Jack to tell Father Roullier in French that I wished to leave so that on our way back to Dai San I could shop for a kimono to give my mother. When Jack relayed my message, Father Roullier held up his hand: "Un moment." He spoke briefly with Niki, who nodded and bowed and left the room. She soon returned carrying a lovely kimono. She bowed and asked me to accept this gift for my mother beyond the seas, a token of friendship between her family and mine. To refuse would have been boorish and insulting. I bowed and said, "Arigato" from myself, from my mother, and from my family. As I took the kimono, I found a fan tucked into the folds. I have it today, autographed by Father Roullier, Niki, Paul, Joseph, and Jack Blake. We thanked all the parishioners for their hospitality and walked slowly back to the prison camp for the last time.

We made little preparation for leaving. We possessed only a few things of sentimental value. I wrapped the kimono and an image of the Prince of Peace that Jacques Poublon had fashioned from the bottom of a mess kit. Major Stokes sent to Father Roullier a message offering him all our remaining clothes, food, and medicine. For the last few hours we talked with friends whom we might never see again.

Then we assembled in columns of four according to nationality — United States, British Empire, and Royal Dutch Empire. "All present and accounted for." The three flags were lowered, and each flag was folded and presented to the appropriate ranking officer. Major Stokes called out, "Right face, forward march." We passed through the prison gates for the last time and marched at route step to the Tobata railroad station. The chaplains brought up the rear, carrying packages of the urns of the ashes of those who had died in prison camp Dai San.

A cold mist and then rain fell, and the sky darkened. Scattered lights came on. At the station the train was ready to take us to Nagasaki. We climbed aboard with very little talk. As the train filled, some of us lowered windows to look out. Suddenly, we were leaning out of the windows and waving and calling "Sayonara." There was a crowd of people from Tobata led by Father Roullier, Niki, her sister Nami, Paul, and Joseph. They all called "Sayonara," and we called "Sayonara," and they called back "Sayonara."

The train gave out a burst of steam and began to move. With the rain streaming down their faces, the people of Tobata sang "Auld Lang Syne." Through the open windows we sang with them. The chugging train slowly took us away.

SELECTED BIBLIOGRAPHY

Baldwin, Hanson W. *Battles Lost and Won: Great Campaigns of World War II.* New York: Avon, 1968.

Cook, Haruko Taya and Theodore F. Cook. *Japan at War: An Oral History.* New York: The New Press, 1992.

Dyess, William E. Edited by Charles Leavelle. *The Dyess Story.* New York: G. P. Putnam's Sons, 1944.

Eisenhower, Dwight D. *Crusade in Europe.* Garden City, N.Y.: Doubleday, 1948.

Falk, Stanley L. *Bataan: The March of Death.* New York: W. W. Norton, 1962.

James, D. Clayton. *The Years of MacArthur, 1880–1941.* Volume 1. Boston: Houghton Mifflin, 1970.

_____. *The Years of MacArthur, 1941–1945.* Volume 2. Boston: Houghton Mifflin, 1975.

Keith, Agnes Newton. *Three Came Home.* Boston: Little, Brown, 1947.

Kennedy, Malcolm. *A Short History of Japan.* New York: New American Library, 1964.

Kido, Koichi. *The Diary of Koichi Kido.* Tokyo: Tokyo University Press, 1966.

Lee, Henry G. *Nothing But Praise,* Culver City, Calif.: Murray and Gee, 1948.

MacArthur, Douglas. *Reminiscences.* New York: McGraw-Hill, 1964.

Miller, E. B. *Bataan Uncensored.* Long Prairie, Minn.: Hart, 1949.

Morton, Louis. *The Fall of the Philippines.* Volume 4 of *The War in the Pacific,* part of *United States Army in World War II.* Washington, D.C.: U. S. Government Printing Office, 1953.

Mosely, Leonard. *Hirohito: Emperor of Japan.* Englewood Cliffs, N.J.: Prentice-Hall, 1966.

Rutherford, Ward. *Fall of the Philippines.* New York: Ballantine, 1971.

Schultz, Duane P. *Hero of Bataan: The Story of Jonathan M. Wainwright.* New York: St. Martin's, 1981.

Shigemitzu, Mamoru. *Japan and Her Destiny.* Translated by Oswald White. Edited by F.S.G. Piggott. New York: Dutton, 1958.

Spector, Ronald H. *Eagle Against the Sun.* New York: Vintage, 1985.

Toland, John. *The Rising Sun: The Decline and Fall of the Japanese Empire 1936–1945.* New York: Random House, 1970.

Tsuji, Masanobu. *Singapore: The Japanese Version.* Translated by Margaret E. Lake. Edited by H. V. Howe. New York: St. Martin's, 1961.

Wainwright, Jonathan M. *General Wainwright's Story.* Edited by Robert Considine. Garden City, New York: Doubleday, 1946.

Weinstein, Alfred A., *Barbed-Wire Surgeon.* New York: Macmillan, 1948.

Wright, John M., Jr. *Captured on Corregidor: Diary of an American P.O.W. in World War II.* Jefferson, N.C.: McFarland, 1988.

ABOUT THE AUTHORS

General Harold K. Johnson, commanding general of the U.S. Army, visiting fellow war prisoners at Fort Snelling, Minnesota, in 1966. Pictured from the left are the mother of Captain W. Bianchi; Bernard FitzPatrick; General Johnson; James Daly; and Burton Ellis. Captain Bianchi, who was awarded the Congressional Medal of Honor for heroism on Bataan, died on a prison ship transporting him to Japan in 1944.

Bernard T. FitzPatrick was born in Waverly, Minnesota, and was educated at the College of St. Thomas, now the University of St.

Thomas, and the University of Minnesota. Drafted into the U.S. Army in April 1941, he was a member of the 194th Tank Battalion, the first armored unit ever to leave the United States to go overseas, in September 1941. He was captured by the Japanese at the surrender of Bataan in April 1942, survived the Bataan Death March, and spent three and a half years as a war prisoner. Among military citations he was awarded the bronze star, two presidential citations, and a prisoner-of-war medal. He was honorably discharged at Fort Sheridan, Illinois, after serving more than five years. His rank was sergeant.

Over the years he has retained an interest in the Pacific war and in Philippine, Japanese, and American relations. He has corresponded with Asians, American survivors such as Harold K. Johnson, who became commanding general of the U.S. Army, and relatives of those who did not survive. He is a member of American Ex-Prisoners of War, Defenders of Bataan and Corregidor, American Legion, and Disabled American Veterans.

John A. Sweetser III, Trinity College B.A., Yale University M.A., was a member of the 110th Tactical Reconnaissance Squadron (Ordnance, Air Corps) during the Second World War. He served throughout the Pacific war from 1942 to 1945.

INDEX